Cover art by Brooke Twohill (Monmouth College '12...one of my awesome recruits)

Forward by Sarah Daugherty (Monmouth College '00...my dear friend who I had the pleasure of working with for several years)

This book is dedicated, with love, to my beautiful wife
Pat, who graciously tolerated my absence from home for
HUGE chunks of time while I was out changing lives!

INDEX

FOREWORD

by Sarah Daugherty, Senior Associate Director of Admission – Chicago Regional - Bradley University

In the field of college admission counseling, very few admission counselors remain in their "road warrior" position enough years to reach retirement. It is not a position that inspires longevity. Even fewer counselors achieve the greatness in the role that Peter Pitts has. Through an amazing amount of perseverance, an extremely quick wit, and a quirky sense of humor, Peter Pitts has touched the lives of thousands of students, parents, high school counselors, and fellow admission colleagues during more than 40 years in the field. After Breakfast, I Change Lives is the story of his experiences and memories over the years, and I am honored to write this foreword.

Peter spent most of his admissions career recruiting for Monmouth College, which is the college I attended. Although Peter was not my own admission counselor, I remember seeing him at open house programs on campus and quickly learning what an amazing recruiter he was. Quite simply, at no time did he lack for energy. The man literally never stopped working. He absolutely lived to talk to students and their families so he could find out what they were looking for in a college and then share with them the perfect bit of information about why they should consider Monmouth. I recall a time when I was still in high school and was shopping at our local mall with my mom. I happened to notice Peter in his customary red Monmouth College sweatshirt and baseball cap, striding through the mall, looking like he was on a mission. My mom and I both recognized him as the Chicago admission counselor for Monmouth, and it was like seeing a celebrity. In fact, Peter often had this effect on people when they were able to meet him for the first time. Years later, after I had graduated from Monmouth College and was working in their Admission Office with Peter, I remember a visiting family who arrived and spotted him. They had been talking with him on the phone all year, but this was the first time they were meeting him face to face. They exclaimed, "Oh my God, it's Peter Pitts!" and ran excitedly across the room to hug him. I think they even inadvertently shoved our co-worker, Michelle, out of the way in their haste. To his credit, Peter never let his celebrity status go to his head too much.

Peter has always been happiest when he is speaking with students, particularly at college fairs. College fairs are large events where colleges and universities send representatives to stand behind tables and share information about their institutions with students and families. Admission counselors typically spend months on the road, dragging a wheeled suitcase stuffed full of college brochures from one college fair table to another. Most of us try to streamline our inventory, carrying large amounts of the most general publications, so we are able to share as much information with as many students as possible. We aim to set up our tables in a pleasing display, with brochures artfully fanned and strategically opened to show beautiful campus photos. Peter provided his students with this general information, too, but somehow, he also managed to zero in on that student's exact interests and would then dive into his wheelie bag to unearth the perfect student newspaper article or some obsolete flyer that no one else had ever even seen. Likewise, his table arrangement would start out organized and beautiful, and by the end of the fair, it would be a complete mess because he was constantly grabbing for different pieces in his enthusiasm to connect with his students. The students loved it. Keeping most teenagers in a conversation (when you are not a teenager yourself) is no easy feat, and Peter will always be famous for his ability to keep people talking to him at his table. Most of us are accustomed to students approaching us slowly, grabbing a couple brochures, and possibly asking one or two questions before dashing away. Many of us require some effort to keep a conversation going with most students, but Peter always made this look easy. I swore he somehow hypnotized them, but to this day, he denies this.

After I graduated from Monmouth College, I took an admission counselor position for another school. Whenever Peter saw me at college fairs, he looked at me, shook his head, and informed me without fail that I was working for the wrong school. I loved my job, and so I always laughed him off. (Peter will tell you this is how I always respond to him.) But I also loved my time as a student at Monmouth College, so a couple years later, when Peter let me know Monmouth had another regional admission counselor position open, I jumped at the chance to serve my alma mater. I'll never forget how Peter chose to tell me about the job possibility. We were both attending a luncheon for high school counselors, and I had arrived first and was getting my materials out of the trunk of my car. Suddenly, out of nowhere, another car came screeching up next to me, and the driver's window went down. It was Peter in his Monmouth College fleet car with its SCOTS license plates, and I sincerely thought he was going to run me over in his exuberance. He shouted, "Monmouth is hiring, are you interested?!?" How could I say no to that?

Peter and I then spent the next 7 years working as Monmouth College's two Chicago area-based admission counselors. I am sure Peter will tell you they were the best 7 years of my life. I don't know if I would go that far, but we certainly had some great times. I learned so much about college admissions, working with students, and life in general from Peter, and I think I laughed even more. We quickly developed a work relationship based on mutual respect, a healthy dose of bickering, and an immense amount of humor. Some of my favorite times with Peter took place during our trips out to Monmouth and back. Peter and I lived fairly close to one another in the Chicago suburbs, and since we were often scheduled to be on Monmouth's campus at the same time, we would travel together. It saved the College some travel budget money, and it saved our own sanity since we had each other to talk to on the long drive through miles and miles of Illinois cornfields. Somehow, I was always picked to be the driver, and then I usually heard Peter dramatically declare that his life had just flashed before his eyes because of the way I drove. At least I think that is what he said. I just turned the music up louder.

I am very excited to see what this next chapter brings for Peter Pitts. He claims to be retired now, but I know he will not let a silly thing like retirement stop him from continuing to tirelessly search out college-bound students and help them find the best college fit for them. He hasn't been referred to as "The Bird Dog" all these years for nothing! I look forward to hearing wonderful stories from Peter as he helps even more students through U3K4College, his college consulting organization, and I consider myself extremely fortunate to be able to call him a mentor as well as a friend.

If, after breakfast, Peter Pitts changes lives, just think what he will do after "lunch!"

AFTER BREAKFAST... I
CHANGE LIVES

V. PETER PITTS, M.A.

You have no idea how long
something you say can stay
inside someone's mind.

Scarlett Leithold

tinybuddha.com

PREFACE

When children are little, when you ask them what they want to be when they grow up, they usually say they want to be a fireman, a dancer, or maybe a princess. When students reach high school age, when you ask them what they want to do for a living, they usually say a police officer, a nurse, a lawyer, a doctor, a business executive, a teacher, an engineer, a psychologist, a social worker, a coach, a professional athlete, or some other popular or mainstream career. Seldom have high school students said, "I want to be a college admission counselor." In fact, in my 42+ years in the college admission profession, I had only had ONE high school student say this to me. High five for him!

The goal of this book is two-fold: (1) I would like college age students to consider college admission work as a lifelong career, and (2) I would like all young people to at least consider (or at least not exclude the idea of) attending a small (usually less than 3,000 students), private, liberal arts college. This book is filled with funny and sad stories...stories about experiences I have had over the years in recruiting students from high schools. I admit I do talk a lot about Monmouth College, a small, private, liberal arts college of 900 students (where I spent almost 28 years as an admission rep),

but there are hundreds of other great small private colleges in this country, and I would be thrilled if every 17-year-old who reads this book ends up at one of these colleges (even if not Monmouth). The bottom line is that students deserve personal attention, great teachers, help, support, opportunity, guidance, and love. Small private colleges offer this in a very special way.

I have retired now...but I am still going to do everything I can to encourage students to consider small colleges. I have a website (U3K4College.com) that encourages students to investigate all the fun and significant programs that small colleges offer. There are already over 200 colleges and unique programs highlighted in this website as individual blog entries.

I also have been giving presentations to high school "college prep" classes. In my presentation, there are two main messages: (1) All colleges are good colleges, and (2) When choosing a college, follow your head and your heart...not the herd! Students need to do a logical, informed search. Then they need to visit their top picks. The wrong way to do a college search is just to go where all their friends are going (to just follow the herd).

College graduates <u>deserve</u> something very special---a lifetime of happiness in whatever profession they choose. I found that lifetime of happiness in College Admission Counseling...and I hope to inspire others to consider this rewarding career as well. Enjoy!

CHAPTER 1---AFTER BREAKFAST...I CHANGE LIVES

College Admission Counseling...

It's an odd profession.

Long hours.

Low Pay.

Hotel after hotel. School visit after school visit. College fair after college fair. Zoom meeting after Zoom meeting.

Driving, driving, driving, calling, calling, calling, texting, texting, texting, emailing, emailing, emailing,...and never really knowing (except for one moment on one day of the year) the fruits of their labor. Even then, they will not know for at least 4 years, if they have been truly successful (since the entire reason students begin college is to graduate from college).

In the meantime, the cycle begins again...and again...and again...until they either quit to get a "real job" that pays "real money" or become totally immersed in the process and do this as a life's profession (if they make it past the 2 or 3 year mark... they are likely to make it a long-term career). There is no end to the process. It is truly a race with no finish line!

(mug available on Amazon. Produced by "Exquisite Mugs" Company)

The Admission profession is a bit like the movie "Groundhog Day"---every year, admission counselors do the same high school visits, same college fairs, park in the same places, go to the same rooms, talk to kids who all look like the kids they spoke with the year before. Over and over and over and over.

I was one of those people---for 42 years! Why did I do it? Am I crazy?

Yes. For sure. Crazy...but in a good way. Let me explain.

There are a few decisions that a person can make that will totally change the direction of their lives: getting married, moving to a different city, and religious conversion are all examples. But one decision that is made by 17 and 18-year-old kids completely changes the direction of their life: the choice of a college (especially a residential college that is away from home). New friends, new choices of majors, internships, study abroad, all new situations completely change the direction of their life. Students are likely to figure out a career path, find a spouse, develop lifelong friendships, and (in most cases) determine where they are going to live based on the college they have chosen. In other words: this decision changes the entire direction of their life.

Admission counselors have a truly sacred duty: to help inform students in this process, but also (and this is a delicate balancing act) recruit the number, quality, and mix of students that the college wants them to recruit. In other words, this profession involves both selling and counseling. The reason I call this a "sacred duty" has to do with the true purpose of our profession: <u>recruit students who truly "fit" the institution...and whose lives will be changed in a positive way and who will be successful</u>. We do not know if we are truly successful until we watch them walk across the stage and receive their diploma. It is especially gratifying to follow these graduates as they live their lives (get married, have kids, change jobs...). I follow over 500 of my "kids" (my recruits) on Facebook. Some of my kids are now over 60 years old...but they will always be "kids" to me.

For those readers who know nothing about this profession, let me give you a brief synopsis of the Admission profession as it was prior to 2020 (the beginning of the Covid Era---which, I am sure, will change the way College Admissons operate). Colleges and universities (2-year, 4-year, small, large, public, private) all have an "Office of Admission." When students go to visit a college, they go through this office. This is the office that processes the student's paperwork (application, transcripts, test scores, etc.). They hire a team of Admission Representatives who each are each assigned a travel territory. The Admission Representatives visit hundreds of high schools and junior colleges to recruit students. To do so, they often attend college fairs (where 30-600 colleges will set up a display table with brochures, etc.) to visit with students and their parents. With most college fairs, there is a strict code of ethics (no "hawking," no trinkets, etc.). This is a very professional group of individuals with high ethical standards. They belong to local, State, and National organizations that help to provide support and avenues for professional development. Admission Representatives communicate on a regular basis (in person and electronically) with students and parents from the time the student first requests information about the college to the day when they matriculate (start classes their freshman year).

The future of College Admissions (especially due to the Covid19 Pandemic) will likely involve more "virtual" and "remote" activities, but the "personal touch" of phone/Zoom calls and hand-written notes will still be what sets apart one college from the next.

In my opinion, in order to truly understand the magnitude about why they are doing what they are doing, new Admission representatives (usually 22 or 23 years old and fresh out of college themselves) need to stay in the profession long enough to watch their recruits graduate. Unfortunately, this seldom happens. The average tenure for an Admission rep is only about 2.5 years. The travel, the stress, and the low pay take their toll, which causes them to drift away to take more lucrative positions outside the world of education. Others move to different jobs within the college, or, if they stay in Admission, they climb the ladder to become Assistant Director, then Associate Director, then Director, then Vice President. Some even eventually become college presidents. Often, the higher they climb the ladder, the farther removed they become from the students they are recruiting, but, of course, planning/leadership development opportunities have their own rewards.

I am more than a bit of an odd duck (I could tell you the names of hundreds of people who would attest to this). I climbed the ladder...fell off the ladder...held the ladder for others...and then finally decided to just watch others climb the ladder...until I just put the ladder away. I was a regional admission representative. There are over 120 regional reps in the Chicago area alone, and hundreds more in other large metropolitan areas across the United States. As Regional Reps, we work from our homes, and our total focus is on the recruitment of students. We live in the recruiting area (rather than on or near campus) so we can be of service to the students on a constant basis. We go to campus from time to time...but most of our time we just stay close to home. Four times, in my career, I was a Director of Admission (working ON campus, in an office setting). Therefore, when I became a regional rep, I certainly knew how to set expectations for myself, motivate myself, and communicate with campus. I had what was, for me, the "perfect job." Every morning I woke up and could not wait to do my job. When I give presentations to students, I always tell them to choose a career that they are passionate about. After all, if you truly enjoy what you do, you will not work a day of your life, right?

One special moment for me came in 2015, when my younger son, Dan, graduated from Monmouth. I had the special honor of handing him his diploma. This is something that is usually done by the President of the college, but at Monmouth, if any employee's son/daughter is graduating, they allow us to go onto the platform and hand them their diploma themselves!

Stories.

Lots of stories.

I have had over 42 years of working with awesome students who have taught me a lot, made be proud, made me frustrated, made me happy, made me sad, made me laugh, pissed me off, and at times made me shake my head in disbelief. All in a day's work. All in a lifetime of work.

Odd kids. Odd circumstances. Funny moments. Sad moments. Helicopter parents. Homeless kids. Goofy questions. Bizarre answers. I have seen and heard it all. This profession would make for a great TV sitcom!

And now, in my retirement, here I go again! I have been giving presentations (at high schools) about the college choice process, encouraging students to at least consider small colleges. My mantra is "follow you head and your heart...not the herd!" I have also worked, on a very part-time basis, as an independent counselor with a few families to help their son or daughter maneuver through the admission process. In addition, I have developed a blog website called U3K4College.com which celebrates all 700 small private colleges. My daily Twitter posts lead students to these blogs.

Have I been a success in life? What makes for success? Let me quote a student who I was interviewing for a scholarship several years ago when I was Director of Admission at The University of St. Francis in Fort Wayne, Indiana. I asked him how he would define "success." He did not hesitate at all and replied: "success is being able to make a difference." I wrote this on a piece of paper and put it on my wall in my office. I still have that piece of paper. I know I have made a difference in the lives of the 2,026 (or so) students I have recruited over the years. Success!

A little bit about the title of this book and how it came to me...
I was giving a presentation to a group of students in the inner-
city of Chicago. The kids in this class were awesome--very inquisitive and bright. One of them asked about how I go about
making admission decisions. I told them that, after they get
all their paperwork in, every morning I turn on my computer to
read files to make admission decisions. But the way the words
came out of my mouth was "after breakfast...I change lives." It
literally just "came to me" as if the words were not even mine.
Then I thought to myself "that would be a great title of a book."
Thus, the title.

After writing 99% of this book, I let it "rest" for a year (after
retirement) before attempting to edit it. I am so glad I did. The
Global Pandemic hit and (probably forever) changed the face
of how colleges function and the way college admission offices
function. Note: the remainder of this book was all written "pre-
Covid19," so please keep that in mind as you read it.

Sometimes, those of us who seldom get to truly experience life in the inner-city of urban areas (except for what we read about and see in the news), we forget how utterly life-changing (and in some cases, life-saving) it is for a young man or young woman to leave home and experience life in a small college in a completely different (in many cases...rural, safe, and peaceful) town. I was on the Monmouth campus (Monmouth is in a small rural community of 9,000 people) one day and I ran into Irving, one of our Chicago students. Irving gave me a big hug and thanked me for giving him the opportunity to attend Monmouth. He said: "I really shouldn't be here." I asked him what he meant by that, and his response was so powerful I asked him to put his thoughts down on paper for me. He basically told me that most of the people he hung out with in high school were now either dead, in prison, or just drifting through life with no direction and no education past high school. What follows are two documents (edited for brevity): the first is his reflections in Facebook the day he graduated from Monmouth in 2018. The second are his words to me in an "essay" to talk about why he "shouldn't be here."

So much has happened in these past four years for me... life is rough, and it is even more difficult when you're away from home. No matter how terribly scary life was getting at some moments, the one thing that kept me pushing forward is my family. I shouldn't have made it this far in life, but it is a blessing to have family, friends and mentors who continue to support me in my journey and show me a tremendous amount of love. This diploma is filled with blood, sweat and tears and I am ready to leave this fall to obtain another one at Southern Illinois University. Most importantly... I would like to give a major shout-out to my Monmouth adviser, Dr. Fasano, who pushed me to not only reach my full potential in the field of Physics, but also to become a competent student. I literally cried when I said goodbye to professor Fasano because it is rare to find a mentor (who, himself was also a first generation college student) in Physics who understands how much weight is on your shoulders and "has your back like a chiropractor". It is time to put this chapter to an end at Monmouth College... a new chapter will begin very soon.

After the ceremony I walked up to my mom and gave her my diploma and said "Happy Mother's Day"

"Waking up in a Dream" by Irving---Every day, it always hits me hard when I am in a class or when I am back at home with my family in Chicago... I shouldn't be here in this moment of my life. If you went back in time and told me at an age of fifteen that I would be a Physics and Mechanical Engineering major in College... I wouldn't believe it. I grew up in the Northwest side of Chicago and attended Public School where there was a lot of gang activity in the neighborhood. After I dealt with so much negativity, all I wanted is to leave the city. As a first generation Mexican-American I grew up with my parents telling me that as long as I put in hard work I could become whatever I want... and till this day I keep their advice to heart. In High School I became really involved with sports but most importantly my community. I always focus on helping others and not myself.
At this moment in time it's 2017 and I am applying to Engineering school and I am scared because what if I am not as competent as other applicants. I never took a Physics class until I came into college. I have placed blood, sweat and tears into the past three years of my undergrad years. As lay in bed every night I would ask myself if I did everything I could today to make myself better for tomorrow. I carry with me on my shoulders my family, community and school and the day I give up on them is the day I gave up on myself.
Science is my career, but education is my passion. I do not have a million dollars to donate to Chicago Public Schools... but I do have a brain. To teachers who are reading this I just want to

say thank you because you are the water and sun to students that allows them to blossom out into extreme heights. There are many issues in Chicago but one of the biggest problems (that shouldn't even be one) is its public education.

Thank you, Mr.Pitts, for everything that you have done in my life. As a college recruiter you go above and beyond especially helping out minorities like myself, from the City, who want an education but are lost or just don't know how. All it takes is an email from Peter Pitts to give a eighteen year old Irving Hernandez hope that there is a school out there ready to receive him and give him a place to call home. If wasn't for you then I wouldn't be able to wake up in this dream that I will never let go.---Irving

By the way...as I type this, I have learned that Irving has found that Engineering is not his career path, but helping his community is. He is now head wrestling coach at his Alma Mater, Foreman HS. I told him that this is a "Welcome Back Kotter" moment in his life...and after a quick Google search to find out what I meant (LOL), he agrees completely. Here he is with his team:

Welcome back, Mr. Hernandez!

*****

Enjoy the little "mini-chapters/reflections/stories" of this book. I have changed some of the names of some students (for obvious reasons according to my lawyer), but all of these are true.

CHAPTER 2---DRIVING THROUGH WAYNE

Routine. I love routine. Routine gives me comfort. [Even in retirement, as I write this book, I have a strict daily routine] Since a large part of what admission counselor do involves driving...I developed certain habits. I might be a tad bit obsessive-compulsive...but as I drove from high school to high school, it gave me comfort to park in the same parking spot each time, stop by a beverage at the same Starbucks, and eat at the same neighborhood restaurants. Once I find a place with good food, clean bathrooms, and free wi-fi, it is my go-to place for life!

It breaks my heart when I see a high school close (several Catholic high schools in Chicago have closed for lack of funding). Visiting those high schools year after year, visiting with the same guidance counselors, etc. always gave me comfort, so their closure cut me deeply. The closure of these schools affects the students and parents directly, but those of us who visited year after year really miss the memories of students we met there and the pure act of "being there." Let me give two examples. St. Scholastica and Queen of Peace. Both are Chicago schools that are now closed. Both bring back a flood of memories.

9/11 hit me hard. Harder than my family even knows. I couldn't listen to the radio, listen to TV, drive by the Sears Tower, get mail from my mailbox without putting on rubber gloves. It hit me hard. On 9/11 I was supposed to attend the St. Scholastica College Night. I always really looked forward to this college fair. Something about Catholic schools (I attended one myself a million years ago), and the way nothing really ever changes there (like they are lost in time) is very comforting. I always had a table (and usually always the same, oddly shaped, table) in the library. It was always hot as Hell. It was the first fair of the fall (always) so it was fun talking with my admission counselor friends (who I hadn't seen all summer). I was getting in my car on that 9/11 day when news came on the radio about the first plane hitting the tower. I turned off my car and ran back into the house. I watched in horror as the second plane hit. When people started jumping from the windows of the burning tower I turned off the TV. It was too much for me. I called St. Scholastica and cancelled. I believe about half of the reps who were scheduled to attend that day stayed home too. I didn't want to venture out. A couple days later, the Queen of Peace College Fair was being held. I showed up early (I was the first rep there), so I walked into their garden (I always referred to it as their "Peace Garden"). I sat and reflected on the true meaning of that word---Peace.

It was tough getting through the fairs that fall (the one at Maine

West HS was eerie...it is in the shadow of O'Hare Airport which was strangely silent due to no flights going in or out). The memories of students recruited from these schools over the years really served as my motivator to move on...

St. Scholastica---two of my very favorite recruits of all time (you will hear me say this a lot...because I have a lot of favorites) are Hang and Sahar. I am still on Facebook with them to this day. Here is a photo of me with Sahar (right) and Hang (left) at their Monmouth graduation:

I visited with them at St. Scholastica (in that hot Library...at that same table) their freshman year, sophomore year, junior year, and again their senior year. They were very successful at Monmouth and now have very promising careers. I am so proud of them. Here are excerpts from an article that Monmouth published about Sahar:

April has been a busy time for Sahar Haghighat, a Monmouth College senior from Chicago. Earlier this month, Haghighat interviewed on site for the University of Michigan's Ecology and Evolutionary Biology program. "This is an international competition, admitting only four students per year," said MC faculty member, Mark Willhardt. "Sahar was flown up to Ann Arbor, along with students from across the U.S. and its territories, in order to interview for her position, and she was admitted into the program."

The biology major traveled out of state a second time to discuss her senior research at the regional Beta Beta Beta meeting in Whitewater, Wis. Also known as TriBeta, BBB is the national honor society for biology students. "Sahar began her 'senior research' when she was a sophomore," said Kevin Baldwin, associate professor of biology, who reported that Haghighat brought home third place honors from the TriBeta competition. "She did an interesting study on the best way to eliminate a non-native invasive plant species from parts of the (college's) LeSuer Nature Preserve." Following the removal of the species, Baldwin said Haghighat found "impressive increases in native bio-diversity."

Queen of Peace---Annie. Again, another of my favorites...and one of very few that invited me to their high school Baccalaureate...then, a few years later, asked me to do a reading at her wedding. She had been my student-worker all four years she was on our campus.

Many others, over the years, from both of these schools have left me with great memories. Wonderful high schools. So sad that they have closed.

Driving home one day from a suburban high school, I happened to drive through the little town of Wayne, IL.

Something about this quaint little village (like a rural oasis in the middle of suburbia) made me feel "at peace", so whenever I am remotely near to that road, I always drive through Wayne. Even now, in retirement, when I volunteer to give presentations to AVID classes, I still make a point to drive through Wayne. It may take me a few minutes more...but it just helps me relax... and reflect on the work I am doing with all these great high school kids.

CHAPTER 3---OH GOD OH GOD PULL OVER

Several years ago, I used to drive, in a van, groups of 6 students to visit the Monmouth campus. We stopped doing this after a while (insurance liability issues), but when Monmouth was just beginning to intensify its Chicagoland recruitment (in the 1980's and 90's), I did several of these van trips. They were always fun, and usually pretty uneventful, but with 16 and 17-year-old kids involved I learned to expect the unexpected.

Art Linkletter (a zillion years ago) wrote a book called "Kids say the darnedest things" (and had a TV show by that name), and wow is that true.

One never really knows what is going to come out of the mouths of these angelic students.

I was driving one group home to the Oswego, IL area, so we were on Route 71 just about 15 minutes from Newark, IL (known "famously" for its BP Amoco/Subway Restaurant...which is about really all there is in Newark). They have bathrooms there. Nice ones. Free to use.

15 minutes from that wonderful gas station...the 16 year-old girl (riding shotgun) turned to me and said: "Mr. Pitts...pull over...I need to squat and pee."

Wow.

Needless to say, I gave her a gentle lecture about the fact that it would be, indeed, much better to wait to use the BP Amoco facilities. Wow. Great material for this book...but still...wow...

Then there was the van trip to beat all van trips. Six students, including "T" and "B" (I will leave their names out of this book for reasons you are about to learn), were on this trip. Unbeknownst to me, "T" had spent the night with one of our students who took him to a fraternity party. I don't think they were drinking Pepsi. Anyway, "T" (again, unbeknownst to me) was not feeling well. Quite hungover (as I found out later).

We were on I-88 between the Quad Cities and DeKalb when "T" asked: "How much farther before a bathroom?" We were a short distance from the DeKalb Oasis, so I told him "twenty minutes." "OK," said "T." "I think I can wait."

It wasn't even 5 minutes later when I heard him shout: "Oh God Oh God Oh God Pull Over". So I pulled over to the side of the road. "T" ran out into the middle of a farmer's field, pulled down his pants, and made diarrhea in the field. While he was out there, three of the other students decided to change the seating configuration. I just kept looking in my rear-view mirror thinking that a State Trooper was bound to come by and wonder why one teen had his pants down in the field and three other students had their butts in the air...but luckily that did not happen. "T" then hollers "does anyone have any Kleenex or napkins?" Without hesitation, "B" (a girl) grabs a fist full of napkins and sprints out to "T." They did not really know one another before the trip...but this was quite the bonding experience. When "T" came back to the van, we said "do NOT touch a thing." So we drove quickly to the DeKalb Oasis with "T" holding his hands up like he was a doctor going in to surgery. We got him cleaned up and finished the van trip. The next year (all the van kids ended up at Monmouth) the six of us got together at Pizza Hut to reminisce about our crazy van trip...and three years after that, at graduation, in front of lots of people...what do you think we gave "T" as a graduation gift? You guessed it. A roll of toilet paper with all of our signatures. "T" is now a successful horror film producer...but he tells me that nothing has horrified him more in life than what happened in that farmer's field.

***

Mercedes---that was her nickname. It was my job to interview her at her high school. I cannot remember her real name (the one on her application), but I made the mistake, when interviewing her, to ask why her friends call her "Mercedes." Her answer left me speechless. She said she was called Mercedes because the boys tell her that she "gives them a smooth ride". Oh my! Note: we did _not_ admit her.

***

While speaking with a small but lively (and a bit ditzy/goofy) group of students at a suburban high school, I was talking about Greek Life. When I mentioned that Pi Beta Phi was the first sorority in the United States (founded at Monmouth), but I really didn't get past the work "Pi." A girl cut in: "I love pie. Cherry pie, blueberry pie, yum!" I tried to ignore her, so I began to repeat the story about the sorority, but when I said the word "Pi" again...she cut in AGAIN: "I love pie. Chocolate pie, peach pie, YUM!" I looked at her said...ok...someday I am going to write a book about all my experiences as an admission rep, and I am going to call it "I lost her at Pie." They laughed. You will note that I opted NOT to call my book by that title...but it was tempting.

***

I was giving a presentation to a large group of students in a suburb of Chicago. I asked if they had any questions and one student in the back of the room (who had been loud and obnoxious the entire time that I spoke) asked about the bathroom/shower facilities. Wondering if we had community bathrooms or if each student has their own. I answered that our freshmen dorms all have community bathroom facilities. "Not for me!" he exclaimed, "I like to air-dry."

No way to reply to that one...

***

I hope this kid remembers that his high school has a library and some classrooms: I emailed him to remind him to stop by to see me when I visited his school the next day. He emailed me back to ask me where to meet with him. I told him "In the College and Career Center." He emailed back that he "forgot that they had one of those" at his high school. Sigh.....

***

Sometimes students say or do something that just shocks me. I was doing a college fair at a large public high school. A student came up to me and I asked him what careers he was considering. He said: "I want to kill people." In retrospect, I should have reported him to the security guard, but I was super busy talking with other students, so I just let it go... I wonder where he is today...prison perhaps?

Another student (again at a large public high school) went from college rep to college rep trying to sell us marijuana. Great little salesman, but no takers. [He should know that admission reps really don't have that kind of money!] Again, I should have reported him to security, but at a crazy-busy college fair it is never a good idea to leave your table. I hope he turned that great sales personality of his into something productive! He is probably CEO of a major company by now!

***

One of my favorite parts of my job is the recruitment of Minority students. The percentage of Minority students at my college has quadrupled in the time I was with Monmouth...and I am SO proud of this. One day, I was giving a presentation to a group of African American students. I had just finished telling them that Monmouth was a small college in a small, rural, farm town. One girl asked what the percentage of African American student is on campus. At the time it was about 6 percent (It is now more than double that). When I told her...the words that came out of her mouth totally shocked me: "Woohoo..." she said, "I can just see all of us hanging from trees..." Wow. So sad that those words have ever been uttered by any human being. Ever.

***

Sometimes what is really REALLY funny...comes from the mouths of other educational professionals. And, unfortunately...to remain professional (and to keep one's job), one must stifle one's laughter. Example: I was meeting with a high school counselor. She was the prim-and-proper (conservative) type. I could tell by her body language and the way she was talking that she was not an individual with a great sense of humor. In the course of our conversation, I talked about all the many scholarships and grants that we offer at Monmouth. She looked at me and asked "Are you well endowed?" My mind raced. My face hurt. I thought for a painful moment and said, "Yes we have about 100 million in endowment," but the whole time my mind was filled with thoughts of all the things I WISH I could have said...if she had only had a sense of humor. After I left her office, I laughed and laughed and laughed... I told this story a few years back at an NACAC Convention (and my session was televised), so many admission professionals have heard this story already. I just had to share it with the rest of the world.

CHAPTER 4---SHE PASSED

T was a really sweet young lady. Full of laughter. She had a heart as big as the world. She visited our campus on one of our many bus trips and absolutely fell in love with the campus. She was one of the first students to apply for admission and was anxiously awaiting our reply. Her GPA and ACT were a tad low, so we requested additional information and a re-take of the ACT. Writing was her strong suit. Check out her essay:

When Ms. C stepped into the class it was quiet, i f a pen should fall to the floor it would echo in the large space. "Good Morning Class." The students cringed. Ironically it was a good morning; the birds were chirping, the sun was smiling, but for the students, nerves crept through every corner and every crack of the room. "Is everyone · ready to read their poems?" Still, silence. The assignment was to write a poem about something, or someone, special to you or something no one knew about you. And for a class of self-critical teenagers, this was a very personal assignment. She smiled, "Don't be nervous. This is a safe space. What's said in this room, stays in this room." For some people her words were a bit comforting, but I was still in doubt. Public speaking can be one of the scariest things to do for many people, but for me it wasn't so much a fear of speaking in public that frightened me. It was allowing myself to be put in a position of vulnerability, by granting people the opportunity to see straight through my 'sugar and spice,' tough exterior, and into my soul though my writing.

Reading and writing had always been something I was good at, but what started out as just a way to get away from the world, problems at home and school, through literature; Personal therapy through writing, turned into a passion. Getting to know the author, without ever meeting them, through their books became an addiction and being able to write my own was a dream.

I began writing in the 5th grade. I was what some would describe as a child in distress, and writing came as a suggestion from a youth counselor. It wasn't long until my writing ability captured attention from my teachers. Soon I was writing speeches for ceremonies and assemblies. I loved reading my work, especially to strangers; they were able to see me as who I was, standing before them and not the 'problem child' image many people refuse to look past.

Sitting there in Ms. C's English class, in front of all my peers, ready to truly reveal myself, brought back so many of those fears and insecurities from the past, but keeping in mind that this was a good opportunity to show people another side of me I decided to take a .chance. Sure, seeing the shocked expressions on the classes face was kind of upsetting but when I was done, I was relieved.

After leaving class that day, having listened to the poems of other classmates who had miraculously found the strength to read theirs, I realized that in that moment my life was forever changed. Finally gaining the confidence to be myself, I, if even for just a few minutes, allowed myself to shine and in doing so unconsciously gave my classmates permission to do the same. As "we are liberated from our own fears, our presence automatically liberates others," (Unknown). This is why I want to later pursue a career in applied psychology or maybe even as guidance counselor, to help people realize their potential by letting go of their fears; later writing a book so that those whom I can't reach personally can read.

So, To Whom It May Concern at the college admissions office, I ask you to take into consideration my integrity, maturity, and other abilities outside of my questionable transcripts, because they were a flaw in my past, and have helped to shape my character. I ask you to believe that I can be a success not only at your school but in life. Thank you!

While we were waiting for updated transcripts and test scores, she visited the campus two more times. She became good friends with the entire admission staff, and would give us each a big hug when getting off the bus. She wanted to attend Monmouth SO very much!

The day finally came. She was accepted by committee decision. I couldn't wait to tell her. That evening, I picked up the phone and called her home. Her mom answered. I asked for T. There was a pause. Then the mom whispered, "she passed this morning." I was stunned. I merely expressed my condolences to the mom and hung up the phone. My hand was shaking. I really could not make any more phone calls that night...I was emotionally a wreck. The next day I called her high school and, sure enough, on her way to school that fateful day, she had a heart attack and died right there on the sidewalk on the way to school.

Our office did not know what to do. Should we send her admit letter...or should we not? After all, I never did tell the mom that T had been admitted. On one hand, it might make the mom happy and proud, but on the other hand it might be like pouring salt on a wound. We ended up not sending it. To this very day, I keep her application and transcripts in my desk drawer to remind me of the absolute importance and value of what I do every day. Yes, after breakfast we changed a life, but even more quickly that life was taken away. We need to appreciate every moment that we have and hug the ones we love.

***

I remember my first high school visit (back in 1977) like it was yesterday! I even remember the names of three of the five students I spoke with that day. B, V, C...and two others. They were students at a high school relatively close to Wartburg College (my Alma Mater...and the first college I worked for as an Admission Rep). I had no idea what the hell I was doing. I had zero training (all too common in this profession, especially "back in the day") so all I knew is that I was supposed to "sell" my college to these kids. The counselor at my first high school visit put me in the gym (we never know where we will be meeting with students...it keeps us on our toes). Then he put the five students on a bench...and gave me a chair facing the bench. I felt like a coach...or a choir director... I started to tell the students all about Wartburg...but was interrupted by B who said "we all know all of this...we have all paid our deposits and are all set to attend your school." Well...that threw me for a loop (especially first day on the job). Long story short, the five students and I had pizza together that night and had a great time! First day on the job and I already learned the secret to this profession: just be yourself, tell the truth, have fun, and be flexible. Nothing is predictable in the Admission profession.

In the course of munching on pizza, B told me that he was "going to be the best pre-med student Wartburg has ever had." So much for humility. Turns out he was one of the best ever...and is now a very successful doctor.

Time came for graduation, and B and V (who had been dating in high school and continued their awesome relationship all through college) both went to the same university to continue their studies---B in medicine, V in physical therapy. One day, V went out jogging...but did not return. Attacked and killed.

My first recruit...my first heartbreak.

CHAPTER 5---BOSA DONUTS

In this profession one never really knows when/how we work our magic. One day (before or after visiting an Elgin high school), I stopped at BOSA Donuts to feed my chocolate addiction. I casually struck up a conversation with a woman whose daughter, it turns out, was a junior in high school. I ran out to my car and came back in with some admission brochures. I didn't think much about it...until a couple years later, in talking with a girl on our campus, I found out that this woman's daughter had, indeed, applied and matriculated to Monmouth. I think it was her junior year at Monmouth when, while home on break, she was horseback riding and the horse threw her and kicked her in her skull. It took a year or two of intense therapy for her to walk and talk again...but she persisted and came back to Monmouth to finish her degree. The year she graduated, President George Bush was our commencement speaker. This girl actually was able to receive her diploma (and a big hug) from President Bush! What a sweet ending to a tragic story... that had its genesis in a sweet donut shop!

***

Another student, a basketball player at a west-suburban Chicago Catholic high school, had applied for admission to Monmouth and had been admitted. One day, while at a McDonalds, he became a victim of gang violence and died; Yet another attended Monmouth for three years, then went back to Chicago to pursue his life dream as a recording artist (excellent rap artist with a couple albums out already)...and then he also became a victim of gang violence.

***

Sadly, as I was writing this section of the book, I learned of a tragic death (auto accident) of one of my recruits from 2008. Her fiancé was also one of my recruits that same year (he was actually the person who "invented" and wore the costume of, our college mascot...so I got to know him really well).

As I was proofreading version 32 of this book (it just keeps getting bigger), I learned of the death of another of my recruits (brain aneurysm). Another life lost. It truly is not supposed to be this way. I am supposed to die long before my recruits die. So sad. Being an Admission Rep is like being a parent to a couple thousand children. We love them all, we wish them the best that life can bring, we wish them success, but more than anything we wish them long and prosperous lives.

CHAPTER 6---PIZZA BOX CONUNDRUM

Road warriors (as Admission Reps refer to themselves) are a fun and wacky group. We work hard...and (especially when young) we play hard. We travel "in a pack (of sorts)" in the fall from one college fair to the next. We get to know each other all too well. Yes, we are in competition with each other for students, but we are also all really just trying to do our best to find the right collegiate home for each and every student. Did Sam once split his pants at a college fair? Yes. Did Marlon start singing/rapping and step-dancing with a group of students at a college fair? Yes. Did we all band together to protect each other when a gang fight broke out at the Chicago National Fair? Yes. (Well...not all...I hid under my table.) There is never a dull moment "out on the road" for those of us who are changing so many lives.

Within our offices, the friendship groups are even tighter. Sometimes we travel together to do busy college fairs in tandem. Sometimes we even carpool back to campus for meetings or open house. Our fellow admission reps become our closest friends, or as we jokingly refer to them as our "work wives" or "work husbands." We spend more time with our co-workers sometimes than we do our own spouses. Sad but true.

I have an "ex-work-wife" who was with me the night before an Open House on campus. Regional reps always stay at the hotel in town, so we were at the same hotel. We wanted to watch a big hockey game on TV and eat a pizza, so we did so in my room. When I stay at hotels, I always like to keep the door open a bit (makes me feel a little less claustrophobic I guess), so we watched the game and ate our pizza.

There was pizza left, so we put it in the box and I tried to put it into the small (motel size) refrigerator in the room. We did not realize there were people outside the door who heard this:

"It won't fit..."

"Push a little harder..."

"Maybe stick it sideways when you put it in..."

"Stick it in really quick..."

"It keeps slipping back out..."

"It's just too big..."

"Maybe if you make a running start...?"

At one point we realized that folks outside the door might be getting the wrong idea...so we started laughing uncontrollably for a LONG time.

To this very day, every time we see each other we think of new things we could have said:

"Maybe fold it in half and then stick it in..."

"Put it in at an angle..."

"It's just not shaped right..."

"Wait until it cools off..."

And so on and so on and so on... Fun times with the work-ex!

CHAPTER 7---OF LEGGE, CHRISTMAS TREES, AND PIZZA

When I bump into a Monmouth alum from the 80's and 90's, there are two questions that start the conversation:

How is retirement? And

What ever happened to Legge? I miss it!

Let me explain.

Back in the mid-1980's, we decided we wanted to have a summer reception in the Chicago area for incoming students. One of our loyal alums volunteered his house (a decision he would end up questioning...) as the location for the reception. When he asked me how many people were going to come, I told him "about 50." We actually had RSVP's that totaled 95, but I assumed (remember how that word is constructed) that we would have a lot of no-shows).

It was hot the day of the reception. Not just hot, but "Hell is cooler than this" hot. "I want to sit in a tub of ice cubes" hot. It was literally over 105 degrees with absolutely no breeze. Humidity 99%. This alum's house was pretty good size...50 would have been tight but manageable. Unfortunately, all 95 showed up. The neighborhood looked like a parking lot. Neighbors were not overly happy with 50+ cars blocking the streets of his quiet suburban neighborhood. We had a tent set up in the back yard, but nobody wanted to go outside under a hot tent.

They all wanted the air-conditioning in the house. So there we were...people sitting on the counters, on the floor, drinking pop on the newly installed WHITE carpeting. People sitting on the toilet stool, on the edge of the tub...anywhere where there was air conditioning.

The reception, despite all this, was very successful. The purpose, of course, was for the new incoming students to get to know one another...and since they were basically on top of each other, they certainly accomplished this task. They may have gotten to know one another too well! (a few dating relationships developed that continued into their time at college).

The next year the alum said..."OK...I will help pay for it, please PLEASE find a different location." We did...and the legacy of LEGGE began!

The Katherine M. Legge Memorial Lodge in Hinsdale, Illinois is a beautiful old mansion in a wooded park on the edge of town. Plenty of parking (it is a public park), a nice kitchen, and just perfect for holding receptions of 200 or less people. Many people get married there, hold memorial services there, businesses hold meetings there, etc.. Here are some photos of this beautiful facility:

In the 80's, 90's, and even the early 2000's we would have annual receptions for incoming students. We would usually also have a portion of the day reserved for prospective students (those who were still in high school) to just learn a little bit more about the college and to meet the people who are the heart and soul of Monmouth.   We would invite (what seemed like) half the college to come to this...so we always had a mini-bus (driven by our fearless Financial Aid Director, Jayne) full of faculty, administration, coaches, etc. that would drive the 3 hours from campus to attend.   We always had several "current students" (who lived in the Chicago area) attend...and many of our loyal alumni would come to this year after year.   Some helped with over a dozen of these programs.

For hundreds of Monmouth alumni, hearing the word "Legge" brings back a flood of memories.   Two of them even met for the first time at Legge and got married.

For me, when I think of Legge, I immediately think of:

Bagpipes playing to greet people

Hot weather (but freezing inside the lodge) Sweating so much I had to bring a change of clothes and wear a sweatband during setup

Ice machine, cookies, sandwiches, pizza in the kitchen

The tent out in back of the building (and the year the tent company did not show up on time...boy was I pissed!)

Wind, rain, storms that always kept us on our toes

The year a fire truck came when the fire alarm went off

Balloons (Red and White) all over the place. The heavy huge Helium tank that we had to use to inflate them. Struggling to keep our volunteers from sucking helium to talk funny...

Shrek doll and cake that were given to me as a surprise 50th birthday gift.

Sleepless nights, months of preparation, anxiety and worry

Sound system that didn't work one year and the lodge employee who called me a "b----" (behind my back) when I asked her to stop making the coffee to fix the sound system

Going to Starbucks after the whole thing was over and just relaxing!

Here are some photos from our 2011 Legge reception:

Anyone who has ever been in charge of organizing a large reception or gathering, knows what a total pain in the ass it is to do so. I could NEVER be a full-time event planner...it is not something at which I am particularly good or even competent. Year after year, however, (with the exception of the year one of my favorite recruits organized it as an internship), I organized this Legge reception. It completely consumed my time from about mid-May until mid-July every year. It eventually became an EVENT that was greater than the sum of its parts...and well worth the time, sweat, and effort. Such good memories.

Alumni used it as a way to "give back" to their Alma Mater in a very special way. Current students used it as a way to see one another again (having been away for a couple months of summer break) but also as a way to help recruit future "fellow-students." Incoming students used it as a way to begin life-long friendship with others (some even became boyfriend-girlfriend...and a few even eventually got married).

The day began in a flurry of setup: blowing up balloons, filling buckets of pop with ice, putting out cookies, brochures, etc....

Then, as guests arrived, we greeted them with bagpipes and sometimes bagpipe drums (bagpipes and drums are a big part of Monmouth College heritage and culture). After some general welcomes and presentations, parents would go one place for question and answer...and students would go to another place for question and answer. Then everyone would go under a big tent (where tables were set up) to meet with professors, coaches, and representatives from student organizations). That's it! Simple, right? After it got rolling, yes, it was simple. However the preparation and organization was anything but simple.

A huge thank you to all the loyal alumni who have helped with multiple Legge programs: Becky H, Ryan D, Becca S, 'Dan, Danny, Heather (the delightful intern I spoke of) and Geri W, Dan C, Jeff B, Ashley and Bobby B, Kevin T, Jamie R, and numerous others. In fact, several of us would meet a week or two after the program over a great burger and some beverages as a big thank you for a job well done.

Here are some excerpts from 'memories as voiced by alumni who participated':

<u>**Heather W.**</u> I remember my first reception as an incoming student where I met some of the others who would soon become my classmates. It was so nice to meet people ahead of time and take some of that nervousness away! Later while at Monmouth, I had the honor of being the first intern to help coordinate the Legge reception and it was something I'll never forget. From our meetings at Starbucks to heading up a committee to day of set up, it showed me my passion for event planning. When the day was all said and done it was so rewarding to hear so many positive reviews from the incoming and prospective students and parents. Seeing both sides of the event showed me that everyone there really did have a love for the college and I felt the same.

<u>**Fannetta J.**</u> I attended at least 2-3 Legge receptions. One as

an incoming freshman and a couple as a speaker/presenter. I think one year my mother spoke about our experiences at Monmouth as well. My favorite memories there, besides the treats of course, include being able to speak about my time at Monmouth and answer those tough questions that students have coming in but think are wrong to ask. I also appreciated being a presence for students of color because I know it can be overwhelming to be in a space that is out of the ordinary in general and feel like no one else understands that experience. I just really enjoyed being able to come and talk about my joy in Monmouth and instill that in others.

Kevin R. I think I attended 4...one as an incoming student, 2 as a current student, and one during the special Big Red (the new college mascot) unveil and (as the "founder and insides-of") the new mascot, being able to do) the "evolution of dance" LOL. The best and most memorable part was sharing my story to everyone from the Chicagoland area...reassuring their parents that Monmouth was an excellent choice and exactly "what college was meant to be."

Andrew W. (Best memory was) having to play (bagpipe drums) for my own reception!! ☺ [author's note: he didn't exactly HAVE to do it...but I did appreciate his willingness to help]

Carolyn S. I attended 3. My first was the summer before attending Monmouth. Everyone was so friendly. After that reception, I literally counted the days until I left for school. Then I attended the next 2 years as a current student.

Devon S. I honestly cannot remember how many I went to. It was quite a few. I thought I was excited going the first time, meeting with people and learning about the college but I think I was even more excited when I was able to return a few years later and pipe (bagpipe) at the lodge and share my experiences at Monmouth with young adults with whom I was hoping to one day share the Monmouth legacy.

Becca S. When I was an incoming student, Dad and I went to

Legge and I felt like it was more a financial aid boot camp for my dad than anything. I looked at the student booths, but I don't recall much about that visit. As an alum, I've loved working on Legge with you. Whether it was running back and forth to pick kids up from the train station, helping in the kitchen, or helping up front with registration. Talking with current students has always been a treat, seeing the love for the school and what path they're following was great. Plus, meeting new people, like Ryan D. (another alum helper) makes it worthwhile. And, who can forget the bagpiper! I would imagine that could be a make or break for some incoming students. For me, it ignites a fire within me every time I hear bagpipes.

Laur W. I attended 3. I loved them all. Getting to see all the future students would come in and carry on the Legacy that is Monmouth College was the best part. My parents came and spoke to the incoming parents about Monmouth college. I love sharing what this place has meant to me.

I really miss doing these Legge receptions. I do not miss all the work that goes in to them, but I miss the warm fuzzy feeling I get every time I have done them. When I die, I want my memorial service to be there. Really. (But don't allow the lady who called me a b---- to work that day...ok?)

I love Christmas. I really do. "Elf" and I are like twins! So, I was so excited when one of our students (and her family) invited Monmouth to hold a Christmas Reception at her home in the northern suburbs of Chicago. We did this for a couple years (in the 1990's). Walking into their home was like walking into Santa's workshop. Christmas tree after Christmas tree...I lost count! We never had a lot of prospective students accept our invitation to attend, but it was always a good time. Most memorable was a bagpipe performance by "Mary Mac." Think about that. Small house. LOUD bagpipes. My ears are still ringing and it has been 30 years!

Speaking of receptions---and speaking of Christmas---I have very warm memories of receptions (receptions for high school guidance counselors) we held 5 times at very fancy locations in the suburbs of Chicago around Christmastime. Great food. Cash bar. We even brought in musicians from the Monmouth campus (in a van or, one year, in a charter bus) to entertain our guests. I would even wear a kilt occasionally. The first two of these receptions were at the Drake Hotel in Oakbrook Illinois (super fancy and beautiful!) The Drake always really decorated for Christmas which really added to the ambiance. These were really fun but very expensive ($7,000-ish), so after the 2014 reception (below photo was taken before our guests arrived), the administration stopped having the programs (much to the chagrin of guidance counselors who had attended year after year and used them as a way to be updated on our offerings).

Many college have receptions like this (one small private college even has an OPEN bar...not just a cash bar...for guidance counselors. We had this reception every other year from 2006 to 2014. I truly believe that these kinds of programs pay off. Student referrals from these counselors always increased. If nothing else, it puts the name of the college closer to the front of their mind! Per one of my favorite (and high profile) guidance counselors: "It made a strong emotional connection...it left a really good impression of an intimate college experience..."

Pizza!

In the summertime, colleges are always fearful of what they call "summer melt"---students who have paid their deposit but change their mind and cancel. What Monmouth decided to do to help reduce melt (since Legge had been canceled due to budget) was to have a series of small get-together (usually in pizza places' party rooms). Some of these were tiny (5 or 6 students) and others were huge (one was close to 100 people). These were all a lot of fun, very casual, and left a good taste in the mouth (pun intended) of our guests. Below is one of my favorite pics (one of whom is a 7 foot tall tuba player---one of the nicest and coolest dudes EVER) from one of these receptions.

CHAPTER 8---BUS IS A FOUR LETTER WORD

To be honest, if I never, never, never, <u>EVER</u> see the inside of a bus again...it will be too soon. In fact, during the last four months of my employment at Monmouth my boss would taunt me by saying "oh by the way, we added another bus trip for you to organize." AAAARRRRGGGGHHH!!!!

There is some history here.

After we stopped doing van trips (because we were growing and needed more seats---plus there are liability issues), we began contracting with bus companies. At first, we did a couple trips a year...then about a half dozen...and at the peak of our insanity we had about 10 bus trips in a year. We worked for a while with the BB (not their real name) bus line...until the trip from Hell. 6:00 A.M. was the pickup time. No bus. I called and they said they were having mechanical problems and would send another bus. Ok. Not good, but manageable, right? Well, bus companies are supposed to clean out the bathrooms that are on board the buses before they send them to a client. In this case, they didn't. Not good. It was a hot day. Upper 90's in the summertime. Imagine riding in a '55 passenger porta-potty'. You get (or smell) the picture, right? To make things worse, the air conditioning broke on the return trip. Windows on coach buses do not open. They opened the emergency hatch on the roof and opened the little driver's window...but this did not help. It had to be well over 100 degrees in this "rolling dumpster." This did NOT sit well with our guests (or with their stomachs). We had to stop 4 times on the way home so folks could breathe some fresh air. I feel so very sorry for those folks. No idea if any of the kids ended up attending Monmouth, but I would not blame them if they did not.

On two another occasions, I volunteered to join our Music professors and two of our music ensembles (Sound of Five and Chorale) on tours of Fort Lauderdale, Florida high schools. On one such trip, on the way down, there was an ice storm in Georgia. The entire state of Georgia has, maybe, two snow shovels and a 5-pound bag of salt (exaggeration intended). Traffic was backed up for over 100 miles. Our musicians even got out of the bus at one point and put on a concert for all the stranded motorists. (Sort of like Woodstock...but in a long straight line). Our bus driver wanted to power through. Once the traffic started to move, we were driving on solid ice several inches thick either side of the bus tires. As we came to Ringgold Georgia, the State Police forced us to exit. No hotels. Where will we stay? Baptists to the rescue!!! The Baptist Church took in about 250 stranded motorists including our group. Where to sleep? Church pews. My back still hurts from that night. The highlight of this experience was the biscuits-and-gravy the church women made for us in the morning. Best B's and G's I have EVER had. Once we got to Fort Lauderdale, the trip went smoothly and the concerts were well received. We had a lot of downtime in the evenings to relax and enjoy Fort Lauderdale. I can still remember having some great conversations, and a few beverages, with my friends Dick G. and Jim B. (two Music professors) and wishing that I could just stay in Paradise and not go back. Fort Lauderdale was awesome. At the end of the concert tour, the thought of riding a bus gave me the willies, so I opted to fly home, at my own expense, instead of taking the bus.

Our regular "recruiting" bus trips (either one bus or two buses) were usually held in conjunction with open houses. No matter how many times we made confirmation calls, it was always a total crap-shoot to predict how many kids would actually show up. The logistics of all of this proved to be quite complex (especially when we had reserved two or three buses). Several times we had to "send a bus back to the company" to save us some money. So many students did not call to cancel. They just 'didn't show up'. So rude. We should have sent them a bill! Grrrr....

The weather was another huge factor. On one trip, we had to make a split-second decision to go or not-go because it was supposed to snow. We made the wrong decision. We went. It turned out to be solid ice, not snow, and the bus had to drive at 6 or 7 mph to keep from sliding off the highway. Then, when we got to campus, the sidewalks had not been salted, so tours of campus were treacherous. I have more than my share of health issues, and I was not exactly a young man at the time, so to get from point A to point B on campus, I held onto two people, one on my left and one on my right.

Then there are the inevitable mechanical breakdowns. Once we were delayed for 3 hours in Princeton IL, sitting at a Wendy's, waiting for a bus to be sent from the main office to rescue us... and another time the bus broke down 4 blocks from where we picked people up. We had to walk back. In the rain.

I took this pic of the last bus trip I had to take for Monmouth:

I hate bus trips. Have I mentioned that I hate bus trips?

CHAPTER 9---MY PAYMENT IS IN MY HEART

College Admission Counselors do not make a lot of money. I always tell people that my "payment is in my heart (not my pocket)." What I mean by this is embodied in the countless times I have heard "thank you" from the students I have recruited. When I posted various things (especially regarding my many work anniversaries and then my retirement) on Facebook, check out some of these posts from my recruits:

Marquis W. ...you were amazing. You helped me every step of the process, made sure I was all set with the financial aid, walked me through the Midwest Scholars competition, and led to me deciding to become a Scot. You are the reason I came to Monmouth College. Thank you so much for all your hard work!

Nikki W. After a friend, Jon W told me about where he would be attending (Monmouth College), I knew I needed to check it out for myself. I thought I would have to make several phone calls in order to get the process started, but once I heard from you, Peter Pitts, it was all easy street!
You called me and introduced yourself as "the guy I would hear from a lot, before the school year started." I was happy to hear from you, and impressed that you were so dedicated in ensuring my arrival that fall - scheduled my visit, fell in love with the campus, and accepted my invitation to attend MC.
I met so many amazing people, worked with so many wonderful professors and staff, and met the man I will marry in November

2017.

I'll never forget the admissions advisor who put my life on the path to where I am now - thank you for so many years of service to your craft - you're truly an icon at MC!!!

Todd H. Thanks to you I had the best college experience a kid could ever ask for and I'll forever be thankful for that!

Frank S. Way back in 1994 I sat with you and some girls (don't remember who they were) as you drove us down to Monmouth. Had a great visit meeting lots of people & realizing how friendly everyone was on campus. Only odd/funny thing was in the ride home - some guys pulled up next to the car you were driving and pelted us with oranges. Only lasted a few seconds, and then they were gone. I'd also like to thank you for letting me meet with other incoming students at various "meet & greets" - always a great time! I loved my time at Monmouth - friends, sports, organizations, opportunities - it had it all. Thanks

Bridget L. I met you at Monmouth during my first and only MC visit. We were standing to the left of the front foyer of Wallace Hall and I was coming out of the student/prospect meeting where they separated us from our parents for a Q&A moment. You said, "Hi Bridget, I'm Peter Pitts. You've been accepted to Monmouth College!" It was pretty cool to hear from my college recruiter before I received my acceptance letter. You followed up with me at least 234,564,322 times to make sure I was going to accept. Finally, I said "Peter, you can stop calling. I'm coming to Monmouth." One of the best decisions ever made. 4 years of fun, education and lifetime memories. Thank you for being consistent with your recruiting and being the reason for so many life-long friendships and memories! Congratulations on so many years of changing lives!

Sahar H. My recruitment experience is what truly sold me on Monmouth College when I was looking for the ideal college/university. Since I always knew in high school that I wanted to go to college, I started attending college fairs both at High Sight (a Community Based Organization that helps students prepare for college) and St. Scholastica HS. Since my sophomore year I remember well that Mr .Pitts, what I called him at that time, was very welcoming. Although I was just a sophomore Peter took my questions seriously, despite me still being on the young side to be at college fairs. At almost every fair I would find Peter and he remembered me and my name. That set him apart from any other recruiter that I met. Peter became a friend and I always looked forward to stopping at his station even though I already knew all about MC (from Peter of course). His kind and welcoming demeanor were comforting to me, especially since I am a first-generation college student. When I talked to Peter I didn't feel like I was talking to an intimidating recruiter, I felt like I was talking to a friend that was looking out for me. He did a great job at promoting MC, so much so that I knew I belonged there. Through Peter's eyes I already knew that Monmouth would be like home, and he was right. My experience at MC was great, I wouldn't trade it for anything. The small class size and individualized attention made my transition from a small high school to college very easy. I remember that I always stayed as long as I could on campus during breaks. I anxiously waited for summers to be over so that I could come back to campus. I mean, how could I not? MC was a safe place where I could be myself and learn about myself away from home, an important thing for an inner-city Chicago kid who didn't feel safe in her city. MC was full of extracurricular activities. It was a place where I could be me, away from my, at times, over-bearing parents who thought that going away to college was not appropriate for girls of my culture. I proved them wrong. My experience at MC made me bloom into the person I am today. Out of the shelter of my parents I learned to become independent and fearless. I learned that if I set my mind to it, I could achieve anything I wanted to do. I made life-long friends there, both fellow students and professors as well as staff. The people I met at MC were different to any other people I had met in Chicago. Many of them possessed the epitome of 'Midwest charm', something not really found in Chicagoans. MC also taught me how to live in a small town and to appreciate nature. It was at MC that I first became enamored with the outdoors. I became so amazed by the natural world that surrounded me that it determined my life-long career of being a forest ecologist. To this day I miss Monmouth. I miss having my friends living in the same hall as me. I miss the conversations we would all have in the cafeteria. I miss the science Christmas trees in HT. I will forever be a Scot and I thank Peter for being the first person to welcome me into the MC family.

Stephanie S. I will never forget the day that you called me to tell me I got accepted! Can you believe that was 16 years ago?!

Christine W. You came to my high school in 1997 and I knew it was for me. I applied early, you called me to tell me I was accepted in early 1998 and invited me to a meet-n-greet to do my schedule! Best decision of my life!

Leah K. You were the friendliest, most outgoing college recruiter I ran into, Peter! I think I first met you at a fair at Carmel HS in Mundelein. Your excitement and joy over Monmouth were infectious, and it made me want to get to know the school.

Samantha B. I met you at College of Du Page my junior year of high school in 2003 at a college fair. You were really nice and spunky, which made me remember you. One million follow up phone calls later, after being accepted, I told you I was going to MC. Loved my four years there, great curriculum, beautiful campus, and best 4 years of my life being an Alpha Xi Delta sorority sister! Thanks for going the extra mile, Peter.

Joanna D. Holy-moly where do I start?? You recruited my brother in '94 and my parents liked you a lot, so before I knew it, you and I were talking about my college plans. I visited the campus with Stephanie O and Christy K in the spring of 95, and it was pretty much a done deal then. Let me just say, if not for you, I would never have met Chris T and life as I know it now would not exist. Thank you Peter Pitts!!!!

Josalyn S. When I was being recruited, my parents wished to talk about financial aid. You decided to come over to our house to sit down and discuss this decision with us. Not only did you help us with the money conversation, but you took the time to tell me about the biology department that I would have been a part of if I decided on Monmouth. When leaving you politely asked where the Starbucks in Tinley Park was because you had another family to meet. After you left, both my parents and I knew that I had found the right college. I can never thank you enough for everything you did.

Todd H. Thanks to you I had the best college experience a kid could ever ask for and I'll forever be thankful for that!

Marleni P. We met at North Grand HS. You spoke on stage and immediately caught my attention. Going away for college was a huge decision for me, especially because I come from a Latino family that did not understand the idea of leaving home for college. You always had answers for what I'm sure were very anxious questions. The bus trips from downtown to Monmouth were also a great opportunity and greatly contributed to my decision to attend Monmouth. College truly changed my life for the best but most importantly it placed me on the path to becoming a social worker. Leaving West Humboldt park was difficult for me but a must! Attending Monmouth College was the best decision I ever made and I wouldn't have done it, if it wouldn't have been for your friendly personality and availability to answer every single question I had. I remember you told me "it's only four years, you will be back home after, this is a one in a life-time opportunity" and you were absolutely right. After Monmouth, I attended the Master of Social Work program at Loyola University Chicago and I have been working for an outpatient mental health center called Pilsen Wellness Center as a psychotherapist for a year and a half and I absolutely love my job. Monmouth College prepared me for grad school and if It wouldn't have been for my college experience, I wouldn't be living the life I am living now and for what I will be forever grateful! Thank you for visiting my high school and motivating me to attend Monmouth College. My brother attended Monmouth after me by the way. I was able to set the example for him and he succeeded there.

Keegan L. It was because of you that I went to college. I didn't apply to any other colleges, and thought I might just get a job right out of high school. But you kept calling my house and insisting that Monmouth would be better place if I attended. My Mom was so impressed by how many times and how tenaciously you pushed for me to just apply. I graduated in 2002. In 2006, I went to Southern Illinois University-Carbondale, and earned an MA in English. In 2010, I moved to Wales to attend Aberystwyth University to work on my PhD, which I completed in 2014. Now I work at Dominican University as an adjunct English instructor. Most of my students are first generation college students, and I hope to show them, as you showed me, that the University is a better place with them there. That each student has value. I don't know that I would be where I am now if it wasn't for a phone call from you.

Jeff S. You believed in me, even though my own counselor said Monmouth was too good of a school for me. Kids that deserve a fresh start and a school to invest back into them. Happy to hear you are continuing to change lives.

Laur W. I remember you saying "If you couldn't be at home on your worst day where else would you want to be" as a thought process for choosing a college. It's a great saying and why I chose Monmouth. Thank you for helping me find Monmouth! I made many happy memories, valuable friendships, and meaningful connections. Monmouth helped to make me the person I am today. All of which happened because of a chance meeting at a college fair. Congratulations on your upcoming retirement. No doubt the lasting legacy you have left on Monmouth.

Leah K. You were one of the main reasons I looked at Monmouth! Your outgoing friendliness and excitement for the school made a huge difference to me as I looked at schools around IL. Thank you so much!! So happy for you and many blessings on your retirement!! You will be missed!!

Katie S B. The most impactful things for me were all the stories you told me of how the professors and staff cared for the students. And how much the school was willing to do before I was even a student. Your care came through the phone. I wasn't just a number.

Jamie R.T. You came to see my high school talent show, and the personal connection is what influenced my decision.

Emma V. Congratulations, Peter! So glad that we met all those years ago and that you helped me on my way to Monmouth College! My life truly wouldn't be the same without you. I hope you enjoy retirement!!

Rebecca S. Thank you for leading me/guiding me to Monmouth and help me to the path that would change my life. I wish you nothing but the best in your next chapter. Any time you want to meet up for burgers or Starbucks, you know how to reach me.

Thea B. Congratulations!!! If it weren't for you, I wouldn't have even visited the campus- and I'd have missed out on the best four years of my life at Monmouth! You're amazing, and thank you

Molly W. Thank you so much, Peter! You are the reason I am in the college that I love! I truly can't thank you enough for all your help and support. I wish you a wonderful retirement!

Megan E. Our 1st meeting changed my life. I had never heard of Monmouth and wasn't considering staying in state until I spoke with you. My talk with you and my first campus visit changed all that!! Wishing you all the best for a well-deserved retirement.

Becky S. I'm so happy for you Peter! You absolutely changed my life with that first 2 hour phone call on my 17th birthday!

Bev K. Peter, you are probably one of the biggest reasons I ended up at Monmouth, my god were you persistent!

Kayla A. I remember sitting down in Starbucks with you and my parents as we went through my financial aid package. You're a huge part of the reason I ended up at Monmouth. Thank you for everything you do and congratulations Peter!

Todd H. Peter, you live, breathe and emulate everything MC I thought is, was and should be. Congratulations on touching the lives of countless people and thank you for making my college experience one that I brag about still till this day!

Caitlin W.K. Congrats, Peter! I have you to thank for recruiting me to Monmouth, and will always appreciate you taking a genuine interest in my future. You've no doubt touched countless lives, and Monmouth was lucky to have you! Enjoy your next adventure!!

Ed W. (I am) at the Starbucks where I first met you to talk about attending Monmouth College! (he then attached this photo:)

It humbles me to read these testimonials. And I distinctly remember meeting with Ed and his mom at that Starbucks. I even remember which seats we sat in. Payment in the heart may not pay the bills, but it certainly makes me a richer man!

One of the absolutely coolest "thank you's" that I ever received was from "one that got away" (a student who cancelled his application to Monmouth and went to another college instead). My phone rang one day when I was shopping at Walgreens. "Hello, this is _____." I had no idea who he was. The name was vaguely familiar...so he continued "You probably don't remember me, but I was the student at Marist High School who always came up to your table and told jokes." Now I remembered him for sure. Not by name...but very few kids ever stop by my table just to tell me silly jokes. He always told me he was practicing to become a stand-up comic. It was at least three or four years after his high school graduation...so I was puzzled as you why he called. "I just want to thank you," he continued. "You told me that your college was not the best for what I wanted to do... so you referred me to a different college. I wanted to thank you because I just wrote a screenplay for a movie that Robert DeNiro is going to be in...and this wouldn't have happened if you hadn't referred me. Thank you SO much!" And then he hung up. Wow.

This proves the ultimate point: making sure a student is in the right place for them is much more important than ANYTHING. It is not as important to reach your recruitment goal as it is to tell the truth and help kids achieve their goals.

Sometimes the thank-you's come at unexpected times. I always try to say "happy birthday" to my recruits on Facebook. One day, when I did so, here was her response:

Emily M
June 14 at 9:59am

The man who changed my life! Thank you!

Thank you so much, Emily.

CHAPTER 10---IT'S NOT ALL ROSES AND HEARTS

From time to time we have an "unhappy camper" (a recruit who did NOT have a good experience who is more than a little bitter). I used to take this personally...but over the years I have come to realize that (a) Even though it is an awesome place, my college is not a Utopian paradise...it is certainly not perfect. Every college has its flaws., (b) it is virtually impossible to ever get 100% satisfaction with any kind of business, and (c) nobody is ever "forced" to attend my college, so, other than introducing them to my college, these students freely chose to attend.

A few years back, I was looking at the messages that students wrote on their graduation caps (this seems to be a real trend these days). Most of them were very humorous or heart-warming ("Gracia Mama y Papa," "Inspired to Inspire," "Game of Loans," etc.), but one of them almost brought me to tears. It said "I will never return."*** Another student (from several years back) posted in Facebook that he "would have received a much better education at XYZ college." Another one out-and-out called me a liar regarding financial aid they were to receive. I think that one hurt the most because I go out of my way to "under-promise, over-deliver, and always tell the truth." I know that 99% is still a pretty good happiness ratio...but it really does hurt. In my profession I tried SO hard...and, in most cases, the result was positive.

One thing I have noticed about the ones who were negative: they usually have had poor grades, social problems, or other "issues" to deal with. Their bitterness about the college is more of a "deflection" or a "miss-direction," of their true bitterness. This doesn't keep it from hurting, but it does help me sleep better at night.

***The "I will never return" girl actually DID return. Many, many times in fact! I had an awesome conversation with her at the 2018 graduation program. She is now a successful artist in Chicago! I call her my "360" girl...not because her attitude pulled a 360, but because of the way our conversations have gone over the years. When she first visited campus (as a high school senior), she was standing talking with me for a long time. She would move a bit to the right every now and then...so I would move with her. Pretty soon we had moved around an entire 360 degrees. Gives a whole new meaning to the term "talking in circles." Hence the running joke that we were "360 buddies." It was fun to do another 360 with her when she came back to see some of her friends graduate in 2018...and it was refreshing to see that her attitude HAD done a 360 as well. With time comes healing, right? Now if I could just convince her to give me a free piece of her artwork...I am so proud of her.

CHAPTER 11---THE TRUE SUPERHEROES

Admission Counselors open the door to a whole new world for students. They introduce them to the TRUE life-changers...the ones that get to know them the best and have the most effect on them: the professors and the entire staff (especially the Student Affairs staff).

Let's talk about "Doc" for a while. The only time I have ever cried during a high school visit was the day I decided (in retrospect, not a wise decision) to talk about Doc Kieft to prospective students (as an example about how close faculty and students are at Monmouth and how much influence they can have). Doc had just passed away---of pancreatic cancer---and my emotional wounds were still fresh. I know there is no crying in baseball, but sometimes, it turns out, there _is_ crying in Admission counseling.

Doc was more than a college professor of Chemistry. He was everyone's friend and mentor, regardless of their major. He was at every athletic event, every music concert, every theatre production. Doc showed up at every fraternity and sorority party on campus. Doc was even, for several years, the official advisor for the ZBT fraternity. Whenever I visited campus for Open Houses, Doc and I would meet for a drink and some great conversation.

Doc was at Monmouth, as a professor, for 33 years. It was just a couple months after he had retired that his diagnosis of cancer came through. Less than a year after retirement, he passed away. Hundreds of his former students packed the chapel the day of the memorial service

I hope Doc Kieft knew how much influence he had on the students and those of us on the staff who knew him. [I learned from him, for example, to put ice in beer. Why? (1) to keep it cold over a longer period of time, and (2) to water it down so that if he had to drive a student back to the dorm, he could safely do so. I also learned from him to NEVER have more than two beers. It is always good to have a clear head]. Mostly, however, I learned from him to be more concerned about the interests of the student, than about my own agenda. I learned to ask questions, to be honest, to be patient, but also to push limits a bit to get the most out of one's self. He was not afraid to tell a student who was getting a B, that they had the ability to do better...to work harder. I do my own share of lecturing to students as I meet with them (I think I learned this from Doc). If a student tells me they have a 2.8, I tell them to work hard to get their grades up. If they have an 18 ACT, I encourage them to re-take it to see if they can do better. Normally, a 2.8 student with an 18 ACT might be accepted for admission, but I don't want students to do just the minimum...I want them to continually try to improve. I learned this from Doc.

One of the Monmouth alums who was strongly influenced by Doc is KK, who is now the CEO of a major international business research firm (at the tender age of 41). I did coffee with KK one day (shortly after he was named the new CEO) to find out what it was about Monmouth education that helped him get to this lofty position at such a young age. His answer surprised me. He said it was informal discussions, in social settings, with professors like Doc Kieft and Mike Connell (a Business professor) that really influenced him the most. It had nothing to do, really, with the course in business that he took (those, he said, can be learned anywhere, even just from a book), but it was the special relationships he developed with faculty, like Doc, that taught him the most about how to achieve his ambitions.

People...not courses. What a concept!

Here are some testimonials from alums upon my asking about "the life-changing influences of professors and staff":

Alum #1 (I learned) The 7 Ps from Prof Connell - Piss Poor Planning Promotes Piss Poor Performance! I have used it in meetings with fellow colleagues, senior level managers, and direct reports - always gets a laugh but always makes my point! One of my most memorable lessons learned at MC, as a Business major, from the late, great Prof Bovinet - his Business in Writing class exposed me to books I now use and encourage others to read in the Business world!

And last but certainly not least - my favorite and most influential Prof McMillan - his Business in Writing course made me the professional communicator I am known to be in my current job today! I get complimented on it daily, and have been the main point of contact for many to review and edit their company-wide communications!

***

Alum #2 Trudi Peterson and Chris Goble... Trudi helped me go from incredibly shy and nervous for that first speech in freshman year to actually majoring in communication with an emphasis on public speaking. She saw the potential in me and pushed it in a way that showed she truly cared. Chris allowed me to be myself even in class with my odd sense of humor showing through in my media work. It was a class I always looked forward to knowing I wouldn't be molded into someone I'm not. Both were amazing professors in the classroom but also outside the classroom... from just sitting and talking about life, to seeing them at other college events, they were 2 who made Monmouth College what college is meant to be... not stopping their efforts with grading our assignments but being there for us in preparing for the life that comes after.

***

Alum #3 Mark Willhardt (English professor, now Vice President and Dean of Faculty) left an indelible mark on me, and has shaped my teaching persona as well as personal endeavors. Whenever I come back to visit, he is someone with whom I look forward to seeing and conversing. From his unconventional manners of motivating students (who doesn't enjoy being berated and mocked relentlessly in front of her peers?) to his shockingly sentimental office chats, this man is a wonder and a gift to Monmouth College. He can always be spotted with his flamboyant vests that match his socks. He is/was a legend and I am forever grateful to have had him. To this day, he is the only teacher to give me a nickname that caught on with other students and professionals on campus.

***

Alum #4 I have to give a shout out to both Erika Buckley and John Salazar (both in Student Affairs). From the moment both of them stepped on campus they have been my two greatest mentors and advisors. Giving countless hours after the official workday has ended or even showing up on the weekends. They have invested so much in me and really helped me develop. They have molded me from a clueless kid from Chicago to a student leader who was able to reach his potential on campus. Its because of their dedication that I am entering into the field of student affairs so that I can be the Erika and John for another student like myself. I honestly would not have made it, if it wasn't for their hard work and dedication. Being willing to listen to my concerns, offer advice when i needed it, and keeping it 100 with me at all times. Both of them are great and I'm glad to have them as mentors.

***

<u>Alum #5</u> My relationship with my college professors was unlike that of most college students. As a grad student at two big ten universities I can testify to that. My college professors were not just professors, they were mentors and friends. Two of them in particular were very important in my life. Both of which have that sort of charm that makes you hate them or love them, no in-between. Mark Willhardt was my English professor for Intro to English my first semester at MC. When I went into his class I had so much dread. Coming out of high school I had been told by my English teacher that I was not a good writer. That thought stuck with me and still does so to this day. Willhardt and his class made me doubt my high school teacher's opinion of me. He worked closely with me throughout the semester to improve my writing skills. His attention and patience did the impossible, it made me not dread writing as much, I even considered getting a minor in it. His believing in me motivated me to work hard. I came out of that class with a hard-earned "A". A grade I am proud of. Along the semester and working close with Mark, he became my mentor/advisor. Mark made me feel comfortable sharing my experience as a first generation student. He became a mentor who saw potential in me and believed in me when I didn't. I remember on one particular occasion during my freshman year, I ran into him at Stockdale after my 10am class. I was walking around like a zombie after an all-nighter. After him jokingly saying and reminding me that "you look like crap" he asked me why I was in such condition. I told him about my lack of sleep and that during my class that morning I was losing my vision. I literally was walking around in a fog. He gave me a stern 'dad' look and told me to go get some sleep immediately and to wait for his call on my dorm phone. That afternoon after a nap, he called to tell me that he had set up an emergency appointment at the clinic in town to get a check-up and that I needed to go. He treated me like he would treat his own daughter. I can't thank him enough. To this day we still keep in touch and I foresee that that will be the case for many years to come.

The second professor/mentor was Kenneth Cramer. This mentor/mentee relationship did not come as easily. To be honest Cramer was not my favorite person in the world when I first interacted with him. Ask most underclassman biology majors their opinion of him and they will have a similar response. Cramer is jokingly known among MC biology majors as "the gatekeeper of biology", at least during my days. His tough curriculum and no-nonsense teaching style culled down the declared biology majors in my cohort from 73 to 13. I struggled in his class to say the least. I struggled so much that I decided to talk to him. My first line to him when I talked to him was "I don't know if you are aware about your reputation in the department...". To which he replied sternly but secretly amused, I'm sure, "Yes, I DO happen to know my reputation...". I asked him if he thought it was worth it for me to continue pursuing the major given my grade in the class. I was fighting back tears at this point, I loved biology so much, I wanted to be a biology major so much. He looked at me and sincerely said "I think you shouldn't give up so easily. Keep going, I think you will be fine." I was shocked. Most students I talked to told me he encouraged them to think about switching their major. His response motivated me so much. It ignited this stubbornness in me that made me keep going and not give up on my major. Since that day I looked up to Cramer so much. I could see what the upperclassman saw in him. He was someone who was very passionate about his field and he expected his students to have that same enthusiasm. I respected that because I identified with it. I was also passionate about biology and it only became stronger the more I learned about it. I still look up to Cramer. We still keep in touch, and like with Mark, I expect that that will continue for many years.

***

<u>Alum #6</u> Laura Moore was and continues to be one of the most life-shaping professors from my time at Monmouth College. When I was trying to choose a college, I emailed Laura, the chair of the chemistry department, and from the beginning she was so welcoming and full of helpful knowledge. During the SOFIA (late-summer paid research program for incoming freshmen) program Laura found out that I had not really traveled anywhere outside of my hometown and promised to change that before I graduated. She puts in countless hours writing letter of recommendation for students to get prestigious research opportunities off campus during the summers (she helped get me into a program at the University of Illinois one summer and the University of Nebraska Medical Center another summer along with four other programs I decided were not as good of fits for me). Laura had a big part in me presenting research at the National American Chemical Society meeting in Dallas, Texas and she gave up one of her weekends to take a few of us Chemistry students up to Chicago because I had never been there before. Aside from making sure I experienced more of the world and the cultures of others, Laura was always on campus late into the evenings and on the weekends to help students with research, assignments, and life. I cannot count the hours we hung out in the student research space working on chemistry, trading life stories, or drinking coffee. Laura also encouraged me to pursue medical school and subsequently helped me get into an early admittance program. Even as a graduate, Laura reaches out to see how things are going several times a year. I cannot imagine where I would be without her guidance and support.

***

Alum #7 Mark Willhardt <u>was</u> Monmouth College to me. He was my advisor, my professor, and an absolute lifesaver on more than one occasion. I was able to go to him for anything, and I knew that he would do everything he could to help me, but more importantly he empowered me to help myself and find my own solutions. He believed in me more than I believed in myself sometimes and that made a huge impact on me.

He was also one of the most passionate and innovative professors I've ever had. I remember one class, 20th Century British Literature, where the focus was "Angry Young Men." Mark had us study punk rock music and lyrics from the 1970s and 80s because he said that those lyrics were just as important to understanding the subject as the books were.

Mark always expected the best from his students and wouldn't allow us to settle for anything less than that. I carry that with me every single day and for that reason and a million others, he remains one of the most important and influential people in my entire life.

Bill Urban used to make you free-hand a map of Europe---a skill I'm still proud of today---as I teach western civilization. It was so difficult at the beginning, I detested it but now it's a skill I use daily. I loved his stories and lectures. It's important to recognize the experiences of those who have come before you and listen to what they have to say.

Roger Haynes taught me how to run, the value of practice, how to organize a well-run track meet, and to let go of things I had no control over. If you respect the value of your team-mates, and work hard, anything is possible. These are life lessons that I now share with my students.

***

<u>Alum #8</u> Tom Sienkewicz (Classics professor), taught me how to travel, make connections, and to think critically. I went with him to Greece. I really enjoyed this trip. I think it was key in shaping the person I am today. Professor Sienkewicz had so many experiences, and he has so much knowledge that, through him, we were really able to get different view of Greece and it's culture. Every day of that trip, I and the other students would sit with him and discuss life and it's curiosities. Through those discussions, I made some life changing decisions about who I wanted to be and What I wanted to do with my life. I also took his Star Wars and mythology class. We had a great time.

***

<u>Alum #9</u> Monie Hayes. I will forever be indebted to her. I used to live for her classes. She always picked the best books and resources. I would not be the teacher I am today without her. Professor Hayes understood the importance of reading for all content areas, how to engage struggling readers, and to think critically about student needs. Through her classes I was really able to open up and understand the different types of students I would have in my classrooms. These skills are vital today. I also teach literacy and hope to Master in it because of Monie Hayes. She also used to sing to us. I loved that. It made her approachable and real. (I sometimes sing to my students too because of her.) She helped to make me the teacher I am today---the kind that puts their students first.

***

<u>Alum #10</u> I remember during an education course that I took with Craig Vivian, we were learning about the different methods and philosophies that we could use to teach our future students. Instead of standing at the front of the class and lecturing about those various methods he actually immersed our class IN them. One particular philosophy suggested that students needed to receive hands-on experience in the environment to learn what was being taught, so he took our entire class over to the garden house's bee hives and gave us an in-depth lesson about honey bees. We learned about the bees and how they gathered nectar from the flowers, then we got to open the hive and study it, and we even got to taste the honey inside! The lesson ended up being 2-fold; I learned a ton about bees in the short lesson, but I also learned that getting my students involved in hands on activities and learning in the environment was a very effective tool I could use in my future classroom.

As I read and re-read these testimonials...wondering if readers of this book would enjoy them (originally fearful that they were too lengthy or too "inside"), I found myself jealous---jealous of all the time that faculty and staff on campus have to develop lifelong friendships with students I recruited. Admission Counselors are a "flash in the pan" to a certain extent. We spend a few minutes with them at a college fair, 30 minutes at their high school, maybe an hour having coffee with them. Then the folks on campus (professors, administration, staff) have all the fun! They get to know the students SO much more than did I. But that is just the way it is in this profession! We all have our role to play. No need for jealousy.

CHAPTER 12---MISCELLANEOUS STORIES (SUBTITLED: "YOU CANNOT MAKE THIS SHIT UP!") GO GORILLAS!

Driving a car at least a zillion miles a year lends itself to some interesting stories. One of my favorites involves a mean dog, serpentine maneuvers, and a colorful boo-boo. It all started on a beautiful spring day. I was on my way from Oswego IL to Monmouth IL for an open house program. I was not in a hurry-...so (to avoid interstates---which I totally hate) I took Route 34 which a lot slower, but more places to "stop and smell the roses" so to speak. About half-way to campus, as I left Princeton, IL, the traffic was really backed up and moving at less than 10 mph. This is odd, because usually I can make the entire trip without even seeing another vehicle. It is also very hilly, so passing other vehicles can be treacherous. I was behind about 10 vehicles, so I couldn't see what was slowing things up. I assumed that there was a farm tractor of some sort. As we passed a farmhouse, a very ferocious and huge dog lunged at my car. I had nowhere to go...so I started to serpentine. Every time I crossed the center of the road I heard a SWISH, SWISH, SWISH. No clue what that was. Too busy avoiding the dog and trying not to kill the dog at the same time. After passing a vehicle or two at a time (each time hearing that SWISH, SWISH, SWISH) I finally passed the vehicle that was causing the slow-down. It was a truck that was painting the yellow no-passing stripe on the road. Oops. The workers on that truck greeted me with a "you are number one" hand gesture. Guess what the SWISH was from? Right. When I stopped to eat supper in Kewaunee, I looked at the car. The entire left side of the car was covered in yellow paint. Sticky, thick, yellow paint. When I got to Galesburg (where I was staying), I had to complete a check-in card for my room. Where it asked "color of car_____" I wrote in: "multi."

On one of our many van trips to/from campus (to introduce students to Monmouth), we were driving past farm after farm after farm. This is rural Illinois after all, right? We even started playing the pig and cow game, where students on the left side of the van had to count the number of cows they saw...and the right side of the van had to count the number of pigs they saw. We were about half-way to campus when we saw a disturbing sight. On cow was dead...on it's back...three legs pointing upward... and no fourth leg. We stopped the van to look. This was before the days of cell phone cameras, so there are no photos of this (unfortunately).

Discussion ensued:

Why a cow?

What happened?

Why is the cow on its back?

How do you even GET a cow on its back?

Why only three legs?

What could possibly have happened to that fourth leg?

In the cow-pig game, will this count as 1.0 cows...or as only 0.75 cows?

The good news is that it really helped to pass the time...and it really helped the students on the van to "bond." In the end, the students came up with a theory that involved witchcraft and a full moon. I stayed out of the conversation.

On another van trip, one of the students on the van had never, in his entire life, been out of the inner city of Chicago. He had never seen an actual stalk of corn. He asked me to pull over so he could touch one. I did.

When I was working for a small college in Indiana that had an AWESOME art department...I was giving a tour of campus to a young lady and her dad. The dad was a very conservative Methodist minister who did not appear to have much of a sense of humor. The daughter also seemed very quiet, religious, and conservative. She wanted to major in art, so we walked around the art department. She asked me where the art exhibits were, and I said "Oh...I know a short-cut...let's cut through the drawing lab." Famous last words. We walked in, closed the door, and almost tripped over the (almost) nude male model who was being drawn by the class. The dad's face turned purple. His daughter's face turned crimson red. I just kept on walking straight ahead.

Parenting used to be easy. Your son or daughter did something questionable...you criticize, you chastise, you punish. Not all parents are this way. One of the girls in my territory came to visit campus for an overnight visit. She was supposed to stay overnight with her (female) host. When her dad came to pick her up the next day, I was chatting with him (he was in his vehicle waiting for her) about her visit the previous day (she had visited with professors, toured campus, etc. and had a great visit!), when she appeared to get in the car with him. He asked her how her overnight went and she said "Dad, I had a great time. I stayed with all the guys in the fraternity house and had a blast!". I expected the dad to be horrified, pissed, or at least a little upset...but he actually smiled. He turned to me and laughed, saying "kids these days!" Wow. Not exactly the parenting I was expecting. Note: we did chastise the host who was supposed to be monitoring this young lady's behavior.

Very, very early in my career as an Admission Rep, I visited rural Iowa schools. Students at these rural schools, it turns out, really work hard to liven up their day to day rural existence by playing practical jokes on their visitors. Who would have guessed? I pulled into a high school and parked my car. The kids in the "shop class" watched me get out of my car to walk into the school. When I came out, the kids had moved two of their vehicles to totally block me in: one horizontally in front of my car and another horizontally in back of my car (about an inch away on both ends). I looked in the window and an entire shop class of kids were laughing their asses off at me. Their teacher thought it was funny too. The principal even found humor in it...but he did help me rectify the situation. Geez. Small town American fun, right?

Speaking of being blocked in...I was visiting Hinsdale Central HS one year. I was running really late for my appointment, so I parked in a space marked "reserved for administration." Oops. When I came out, the person whose spot I had taken parked directly behind me (pinning me in) and wrote a nasty note and stuck it on my windshield. I was in a hurry for my next appointment, so I drove up ON to the sidewalk...drove down the sidewalk...and back on the street. VICTORY (but lesson learned... don't piss off school administrators ...sometimes a good parking space is the only bright spot in their day).

One time, at a college fair, two females came up to my table. You know how some older people look young...and some younger people look old? Yup. I referred to the one girl as "your mother"...turns out they were both 17 years old. Oops.

When I was the Director at Lindenwood College in Missouri, there was a young lady who was denied admission. She knew she was denied, but was afraid to tell her mom. So she packed up all her belongings to move into our dorm and drove with her mom to Lindenwood on move-in day. I don't know what was going through her head ("perhaps if I just show up they will take pity on me and let me move in?") but I called her in to my office and told her she and all her belongings would have to just go back home with her. She cried and refused to leave my office. I had to call Security to come remove her from my office. In the meantime, I went to the lobby to give the bad news to the mom. So sad. I have always wondered how the conversation went on the ride home.

At that same college, I had the task (as Director) to interview a student whose grades were very low. I was looking at the transcripts he had handed to me. I noticed that he was your basic C/D/F student. We talked a bit about his need for academic improvement. Then I turned over the transcript to the side with the test scores. ACT test scores are on a scale of 1 to 36, with the National average being about 19. Given his grades, I was expecting perhaps a 15 or 16 ACT.

He had a 7. In a shocked voice (and probably a bit too loudly) I exclaimed: "a SEVEN???!!!!"

"Mr. Pitts"...he meekly said in a very hurt way..."you could have been a little nicer about that..." And you know what? He was 100% right. I was very insensitive and learned a lot, from that incident, about finding out more about students before rushing to a conclusion. This reminds me of a story I heard from one of my colleagues. She is a guidance counselor at a high-profile high school. She met with a parent of a student who was well into the bottom half of the class academically. When the counselor told this to the mom, the mom said "well I knew Johnny wasn't in the top half of the class, but I had no idea he was in the bottom half." (things that make you go "huh?") My grandmother was right: the nut doesn't fall very far from the oak tree.

The first few years I was with Monmouth, I had the honor of accompanying our choirs on a tour of high schools in Fort Lauderdale Florida. Tough job, right? Anyway, while I was there, I received a note from a student who lived about three hours from Fort Lauderdale asking if he and his mom could drive over to Fort Lauderdale to meet with me about Monmouth. We set a day and time. When they arrived, we spoke for about 20 minutes when he asked the question: In what part of New Jersey are you located? (there is a Monmouth University in New Jersey...no relation to my Monmouth College of Illinois). They had just drive 6 hours (round trip) to visit about the wrong college. That is another conversation (on the return trip) that I have often wondered about.

I know enough Spanish to get me in trouble. Yo comprendo mucho mas que puedo hablar, ok? Anyway, I met with a student and their parents at a Starbucks. The student had to translate for the parents who spoke no English. I told the student that it was "ok" to have a car on campus as a freshman. The way he translated it, in Spanish, was "Mr. Pitts says I <u>have</u> to have a car on campus." He was shocked when I corrected him, he said "I thought you didn't speak Spanish." Si. Puedo yo comprendo un poco. I cannot believe what kids think they can get away with.

College Fairs can go one of two ways: they can be really really busy...or they can be very slooooooooooow. One fair had a LOT of college reps that showed up...but only a couple students. So....since the guidance director had bought about a zillion pizzas for the kids and the reps, all the admission reps got to not only eat themselves sick on pizza, but also go home with a an entire pizza or two. Great job perk! Another fair had a lot of kids show up, but (well) only ME as the rep (4 colleges signed up to attend, but 3 of them cancelled). I was SO popular that night (by default)!

Speaking of college fairs, whenever the Ivy League colleges show up, the line to see them is very lengthy. Parents are so proud to see their youngster being interviewed by these "prestige college" reps. Here is a quick note from one of my fellow reps about this: This spring, at the Hinsdale fair, I was situated next to Yale, as always. A young man approached the rep and struck up a conversation. Out of the corner of my eye, I noticed his mom. She had a camera with a two foot telephoto lens, taking pictures of the poor kid talking to the rep.

I hope she got some great photos.

Another interesting (and irritating) thing that happens at college fairs occurs due to the "perception of value" of colleges that are very popular and well-known. I call this phenomena "roadblock." Long lines of students form at these "popular" colleges that literally block the traffic in the aisles between the rows of colleges. Students, it appears, would rather wait in line for 25 minutes to talk to the college that probably isn't a good fit ("but who cares...my parents and friends will be so proud of me when they hear I am going there")...than spending that time talking with colleges that might actually be a perfect fit for them (but now they will never know). In the meantime, 80% of the college reps at a given college fair only talk with a handful of students (or sometimes even zero). I wish students would be less concerned with status and popularity...and more concerned with "fit."

I work a lot with our wonderful alumni. Many of our alumni go way above and beyond in terms of helping us recruit students. There are times when the laws of physics prohibit me from being in two places at the same time. Come to think of it...that would be _every_ time. Anyway, one time is especially memorable. Dan Cotter (who is mentioned several times in this book) is one of our most active alumni supporters and a Trustee of the college. He has made phone calls, emailed, chaperoned our bus trips, and done a myriad of other really helpful things. One of those things involved doing a college fair that I could not get to...which means he needed to get a Monmouth table covering, brochures, inquiry cards, etc.. Dan works in the Loop in downtown Chicago. It just so happens that a couple days before he was going to cover the fair for me, I was in the Loop as well (but without my car). I waved-down a taxi and climbed in with the briefcase (containing all the admission materials). Dan was going to meet me on the corner of Adams and Federal. I instructed the driver (who seemed very suspicious of my actions) to drive me to that intersection. When we got to that corner, I told the driver to just pull up and let me hand the briefcase to "that man in the trench coat." Dan was actually wearing a trench coat. The driver looked very nervous. Obviously he didn't want to be an accessory to a crime (what looked like a major drug deal to the casual observer). When we sped away from that intersection, the entire way to Union Station, the driver did not want to talk to me or listen to my explanations. He just wanted to get rid of me. Funny as hell!

My last name is Pitts. You would not believe how many people spell this incorrectly...and not exactly in a politically correct way. A few years ago, we received an envelope from a Chicago high school addressed to: Peter Titts, Monmouth College, 700 E Broadway, Monmouth, IL 61462. Sigh. This is not the first time. When I was Director of Admission at St. Francis in Fort Wayne, Indiana, I received a letter that was personalized... so my name appeared not only in the address, but at least once in each paragraph. Mr. Titts appeared at least 8 times in the letter. My secretary was laughing SO hard. (Please, folks...get my name right, ok? Geez.)

Also, while at St. Francis, we attended a downtown "fair" of sorts to promote the college. One homeless gentleman picked up an application form from our table. Three days later it arrived in the mail. Filled out in pencil. Nothing spelled correctly...but the totally gross thing was there was (in the upper left-hand corner) what appeared to be a human booger with a hair attached to it. My secretary (the same one mentioned above) brought it to me in a plastic baggie with a note that said: What am I supposed to do with this application? Note: we destroyed it. Grossest thing that ever landed on my desk. By far.

Speaking of landing on my desk. Also when I was Director at another college, there was a girl we had recruited from Boston. I even did a home visit with her family when I went on an East Coast trip. She walked into my office one day and put a razor blade on my desk. Pointing to her neck she said "this time I am going to do it right." Wow. I have not been trained for this is all I could think. We closed the door and talked. I then took her to a local hospital where she was treated...and the spent several weeks at a rehab facility. All my stories are not funny...this one was so sad, but had a happy ending. She got her college degree and was able to get her life back together.

On a much lighter note....

As I said, my last name is Pitts. My college is Monmouth. Our mascot: Big Red (we are the Fighting Scots). So imagine my confusion and laughter upon reading this email from a very confused young lady:

Hello Peter,

I want to say thank you for helping me for the last 6 months and it's been a pleasure applying to Pittsburg State University and I hope everything in the future will be a success. Thanks for asking any questions that I may have ask to get me a better understanding of things. Thanks for naming the mascot my favorite animal Gorilla. I will not be attending Pitts state.

Go Gorillas!!

CHAPTER 13---MY LIFE AS AN ANGEL

I am not an overly religious person...but I do view myself as a spiritual person. All too often (and sometimes I can even feel it happening) this is something very "other-worldly" that occurs with a chance encounter. Almost as if it was "destiny" that brings a student to my table...or to apply for admission...etc. Example: I was sitting at Lane Tech HS in their college resource center, waiting for students to come to my table to learn about my college. I was not getting any takers...so I struck up a conversation with Thea. Thea was a student sitting about 6 feet behind me...just trying to eat her lunch (in peace) but this old man (me) ended up talking her ear off about Monmouth. She was interested. Very interested. It turns out she not only came to Monmouth, but she became one of our top student athletes (awesome runner) and I consider her to be one of my favorite recruits of all time. Why was she at that location? Why did I strike up that conversation? Was this just something at was "meant to be" or was I just lucky? Is it luck or is it fate?

Another example is in a testimonial statement by one of my recruits:

"Having high functioning autism, I knew that I wanted to go to a small school. I just never knew that schools could be this small. Monmouth was 1,100 students when I enrolled. That is one-third the size of my high school when I graduated. When I first met Peter Pitts, I didn't realize I had just met the man who was going to change my life forever. I remember walking up to his booth at a college fair at my high school and simply saying "Oh, I see you have theatre as a major!" And he gave me the contact information for the head of the theatre department. I didn't know it then, but everything that had happened in my life had been leading up to this moment. I'm not a religious person, but I truly believe that some higher power had led me to that booth, to that man, to my future. Call it what you want, destiny, fate, whatever. Peter Pitts was the reason I met my boyfriend, the reason I made so many close friends, the reason I found a club I absolutely love being a part of, and the reason my life is on the right track. Thank you for everything, Mr. Pitts. I truly can never thank you enough for all that you did for me."

An even "other worldlier" example brings me to the Mother McAuley college fair many years ago (late 80's or early 90's). This is always a super busy college fair, and I was about all talked-out by 9:00pm. I packed my bag and sprinted toward the door. At the door was Sister Kate (one of their counselors at the time). I turned to her and asked: "do you have any bagpipers this year?" Now this is not a question I usually ask. In fact, since they do not have a bagpipe band, I wonder to this very day why I asked the question. I mean really---all I wanted to do was get in my car, listen to music, and drive home. What possessed me? "Yes," said Sister Kate..."Kate B is a bagpiper and is looking for a college that has bagpipe scholarship opportunities." Long story short...I made an appointment to meet with her, then she attended Monmouth for four years on a bagpipe scholarship, and is now one of our proud alumni. She even has helped me out with piping for some of our Chicago area functions. One day I asked Sister Kate why <u>she</u> thought that I asked that question that night. She just smiled and pointed to the sky.

I truly believe that if "it was meant to be...it will be." One day, I was visiting Oswego High School. I was a bit lost (inside the building) and ended up cutting through the library. In the library was Natalie H, a senior...just trying to study. She was wearing an "Iowa" sweatshirt (I received my Masters at the University of Iowa), so I just casually struck up a conversation with her. She said she was probably going to enroll at Iowa. I did not press the issue, but I did talk with her a bit about our great Education major at Monmouth. She applied, was admitted, visited, and graduated 4 years later and is now a teacher in the suburbs of Chicago. What caused me to strike up this conversation? Natalie's life was completely changed because of that brief encounter in a school library.

Stephanie O was all registered to go to Monmouth University (New Jersey), so when her friend Joanna D (an entering Monmouth student) asked me to show the two of them around campus one day, I really wasn't trying to "sell" anyone anything. As far as I knew, I was just helping Joanna show her friend what Monmouth College (of Illinois) was like. At the end of the tour, Stephanie turned to me and asked for an application for admission. The rest is history. She was one of the best athletes we have had and we are Facebook friends to this day. So much for New Jersey, right?

I am known for being able to keep students at my table (at college fairs) for a very long time. My fellow recruiters from other college always ask me how I do it and this is what I tell them: The longer you talk (not about the college...but about THEM), the higher the chance of actually recruiting the student. If you can get on the same "wavelength" as the student...if you learn as much as you can about their interests and passions...if you try to find out what is really most important to the student...if your personalities just "click"...then the students will remember you, they will remember the college, and they will likely visit and apply. The college visit is crucial, but piquing their interest at a college fair is the way everything sometime begins. I call it "almost hypnosis." It is not really hypnosis in the clinical sense, but it is the ability to get on a student's "wavelength" and convince them to at least consider my college. With great power, comes great responsibility, right? So I do a LOT of refer-ring students to other colleges. Honesty and sincerity goes a long way to become a responsible angel!

I remember vividly, at the last college fair of my 42 year career, just before retiring, meeting Victor and Maeve. Victor was a junior and his friend Maeve was a sophomore. The conversation just "clicked"---we were "in the zone"---I just know that both of them will visit and apply. It was a memorable way to end my career.

CHAPTER 14---IT TAKES A VILLAGE

Juan is one of the students who decided to come to Monmouth.

Let's examine how many people it took to get him there.

Duane, Trent, and Nick designed the brochure that piqued Juan's interest. It is what drew his eyes to the table at a college fair. The folks at Kellogg's Printing made the brochure look awesome.

Brandon is the admission representative who spoke with him and made him even more interested in Monmouth.

Lori is the secretary who input Juan's name into the computer system so that he would receive mailings from us.

Kellogg's Printing along with Dana from the Admission Office, made sure that Juan received regular correspondence from us.

Juan decided to visit the campus, so he did the online sign-up to attend the bus trip to visit our campus. Michelle collects all these reservations.

Iris and Peter make sure that his visit is confirmed and that Juan knows what time to meet the bus.

On the day of the bus trip, Steve (who has driven coach buses for us for over ten years) makes sure our guests are treated well and get to campus safely.

Prior to the Open House, Mark and the entire maintenance staff made sure that our facilities looked great for Juan. Juan's first impression was a lasting impression, and a good one!

Michelle, Sarah, Jess, Sommer, and the rest of the Admission Staff check Juan in for the Open House and make sure he has a good visit.

Johnny (one of our student ambassadors) gave Juan a tour of campus that was a lot of fun...and super informative.

Juan is a soccer player, so Kooten, our soccer coach, spends some quality time with Juan to talk about our soccer program.

Juan is debating between Biology and Business as majors, so he visits with Laura and Mike (professors in each of those areas) about what we have to offer.

Kim and the rest of the food service staff prepared lunch for Juan and the rest of our visitors. Awesome food.

After the visit, Juan applied for admission online.

Heather processed the application, Peter and Iris kept in touch with Juan all through the process.

One day Juan is at the mall wearing his Monmouth T-Shirt. One of our alums, Dan, stops and give a great testimonial for his Alma Mater.

Juan's guidance counselor, Adrianna, also has visited our campus and tells Juan that his decision to attend Monmouth was a good one.

Juan attends registration/orientation and meets Jim and all the other Student Affairs folks...and a large group of upperclassmen

On Matriculation Day (the first official welcome to campus in the fall), Juan meets Clarence (our President) and shakes hands with countless faculty.

Have you lost track of the numbers yet? It literally takes a village to recruit a student. Note: it may take a village to recruit a student, but it only takes ONE bad encounter/experience to lose that student. As my old boss Dick Valentine used to say... you have to "sweat the small stuff." All these people who get involved in the process help us with all the little details that make for a perfect experience for each student we recruit.

Help from our alumni is a "special kind of help." The selflessness and loyalty of our Monmouth alumni is beyond amazing. The entire W family would be a good example of this. Dan and Geri W met at Monmouth and got married shortly after graduation. They had two children: Danny and Heather. I had the honor of being Heather and Danny's admission representative. Dan and Geri helped us in SO many ways over the years: referring students to us, helping with our annual Legge reception in Hinsdale, making phone calls for us, and even helping me with my coffee-shop visits with students' families. Dan is a retired lawyer and judge. He has helped me in correspondence with students interested in Pre-Law, he has come to campus to help our current Monmouth students in a mock trial situation (we call it Moot Court), and in numerous other ways. When Danny and Heather were current Monmouth students (and then when they were alums), they joined in an helped with these things as well.

There are hundreds of Monmouth alums who have helped our office over the years. One has paid for many of the bus trips we have done, several have opened their homes for student receptions or paid for receptions at restaurants. Many have made calls, helped with college fairs, written notes to students, referred students, etc..

We are so thankful and grateful or their generosity, loyalty, and support.

CHAPTER15---WE ALL WEAR WINGS

Admission representatives only one part of a larger community of angels. In addition to high school counselors, there is a whole group of individuals that work for Community Based Organizations who totally change the lives of students on a day to day basis.

I do a LOT of inner-city work, with students who are absolutely awesome, but they come from challenging backgrounds. Parents who are divorced or in prison. Homeless. Food challenged. Victims of gang violence. Extremely low income. Working with these students is one of my favorite parts of my job. These students are really hungry for success, and truly motivated to make a life for their family that is positive and uplifting. As I read their essays, I am continually amazed with the resilience shown by these students.

Community Based Organizations exist for one purpose and one purpose only: to make sure these inner-city students have a future that includes a great college education. In Chicago, some of these organizations include: AVID, OneGoal, Gear Up, Chicago Scholars, High Sight, Daniel Murphy Scholarship, LINK Unlimited, MetroSquash, Genesys Works, College Possible, Mikva Challenge, and LaunchU. Most are not-for-profit organizations staffed by some of the most dedicated individuals I have every had the privilege to work with. We (as college Admission reps) work hand in hand with the counselors/teachers at these agencies. We could never do what we do without the help and support of both high school guidance counselors and these CBO counselors.

Let me give you a perfect example. High Sight is a CBO that was begun by Mark Duhan about 20 years ago.

High Sight raises money to fund partial scholarships to enable low income students to attend private (mostly Catholic) high schools in Chicago. Over the years, Mark and his fellow angels from High Sight have touched the lives of hundreds of young people. They have not only changed lives...they have SAVED lives.

Patty is a very special angel. You could ask ANY graduate of High Sight "who embodies the heart and soul of High Sight?" and they would all say "Patty!" I am proud to say that I have worked with Patty, Mark, Maggie, Dean, and the rest of these awesome people for close to the entire 20 years that they have been in existence. Patty, Mark, Maggie, Dean (and others) push the students to be the best they can possibly be. They tutor. They teach. They send the kids to an "Out East" private school in the summer to teach them what the world is like outside of Chicago. They are tough. They demand a lot. They make the kids learn how to speak in front of groups. They make the kids learn to write well. In the end, 100% of their kids (20 to 40 a year) go to college and go on to be very successful. They follow them through their college years. They attend their college graduations. They keep in touch with them for LIFE! It takes a special group of angels to touch, change, and save as many lives as the High Sight organization does.

My last visit to High Sight before my retirement was a very special visit. I got there early. When Patty saw me she raced to the closet and closed the door. I thought that was odd. Anyway, toward the end of the program (there were about 100 students and 16 colleges at tables in the room), Patty asked the people for their attention. She totally shocked me with a beautiful thank you note written by the students, a nice gift, some balloons, and a beautiful cake. I am so not worthy!

CHAPTER 16---THE GREATEST COMPLIMENT OF ALL

We were on our way back from campus in a 7-passenger van. Yvette V was in the back of the van. She hollered from the back of the van: "Mr. Pitts you can stop calling me now...I am coming to Monmouth for sure. No more calls!!!!!" Back in the day, I had quite the reputation for making tons of phone calls to students. That was before social media and texting took over the world (and my voice went to hell). Yvette was really an awesome student. Any college would have loved to have her. What a tremendous artist! Her artwork was all over campus, including page 8 of the literary magazine that we publish every year. When she graduated from Monmouth, I asked her to autograph one of her pictures, so she wrote: NO MORE CALLS XOXO, YVETTE. I still have this picture!

Landscape Acrylic on masonite

Yvette Claudia Velez

No more phone calls! XOXO, Yvette Claudia Velez

Guess what her first job was out of college? Yup...a college recruiter. LOL Now it was HER turn to make zillions of calls to students. Ironic, right? Turnaround is fair play. Karma wins again!

The greatest compliment of all is to recruit students who follow in your footsteps and go into the same profession. Very heartwarming to see this happen. Here is a partial list. I am sure there are more.

Jimmy S---Jimmy even showed up on the front cover of Parade Magazine one Sunday. The issue was the one that talked about salaries about people in different professions. Jimmy was in there as an admission representative...with his salary (a very low one) listed.

Katie S---Katie helped me with a LOT of admission functions (including our big Legge program that I spoke of earlier in this book). Upon graduation, one of the things she has done has been to function as Director of Admission for an online university. Now she is a very successful realtor in the Hinsdale IL area. Ironically she said this, recently, on Facebook: "If you enroll, I will stop calling ◆◆ No, I'm kidding. I mean you did say that, but the most impactful things for me were all the stories you told me of how the professors and staff cared for the students. And how much the school was willing to do before I was even a student. Your care came through the phone. I wasn't just a number." When she was with the online college, she too made zillions of calls to students. Karma.

Mike D---Mike and I were virtually joined at the head (almost literally) for a few months while I was recovering from a broken wrist. He became my driver, my helper, and my apprentice. He was my "mini-me." I am so thankful for his help. I truly admired his passion about helping students with their futures. He then determined that this was the perfect profession for him to pursue. Check out this note I received in 2020 from Mike:

"Peter Pitts was an inspiration to pursue higher education as a career path, specifically admissions recruiting. I spent three months being Peter's assistant, doing the "heavy lifting" that he could not do because of his broken wrist. This included, but not all, driving to schools, college fairs, ordering Starbucks and carrying his "luggage" (pamphlets, etc.). During this time, I also was beginning graduate work, but quickly realized that my passion was to inspire students to choose the college or university which fits them as a person. I had graduated from Monmouth with a Mathematics degree, with no idea what I wanted to do with my life. This experience truly inspired me to begin a career working in admissions/recruiting/marketing of college students. Following my time with Peter, I spent two and half years at a similar small college, Buena Vista University in Storm Lake, Iowa. There I was promoted to Senior Admissions Counselor. The passion and tutelage from Peter translated into my own personal "style" of recruiting. He taught me that I could be myself while also portraying my passion for higher education, while also promoting the college I was recruiting. This proved very successful during my tenure at BVU. I continued to keep in contact with Peter this time to bounce ideas of one another and seek advice to improve my craft. The advice of being yourself inspired me to continue my passion and continue in a similar role at Jacksonville University in Jacksonville, Florida, where I currently reside. In this role, I not only assisted with recruiting efforts, but also worked directly with the Dean of the Business School to create recruitment materials and formulate a rebranding effort in hopes of boosting enrollment. While I am not currently working in higher education full-time anymore, I currently serve as an adjunct instructor of development mathematics at Florida State College at Jacksonville. I am currently searching for a PhD program to become a full-time professor. My passion for inspiring and affecting college students' lives continues on through my current instruction. I couldn't express my appreciation to Peter enough, as he is truly an inspiration and cared about his recruits even after they enrolled. I see him as a role model of a professional I aspire to be. Between his unique personality quirks, sayings, and puns alike, there will never be a person who could live up to the legacy of Peter Pitts."

Andrew W---Andrew is another one of my favorites! From the first time I met with him for coffee at Starbucks by Woodfield Mall in Schaumburg IL...through the times he helped with our Legge reception (including playing bagpipe drums at his own reception...when he was really supposed to just be a guest)... through the times I watched and listened to him and the rest of our awesome Pipe Band play at football games, graduations, etc...he was always the loyal Fighting Scot! He even studied for a semester in Scotland where he met his wife (she was the daughter of his host family!) So imagine my pride and my surprise to see him on the road as an admission representative for a music college. He even referred countless students to my table when they showed an interest in a major that his college did not offer.

Alicia M---I remember talking with Alicia first at St. Benedict HS where she went to high school. I kept in touch with her during her four years at Monmouth, then (upon graduation) she joined our admission staff as a recruiter. It was so much fun working side by side with one of my own recruits. She later switched to the other side of the desk (as we say) to become a high school guidance counselor.

CHAPTER 17---GOING THAT EXTRA MILE

If there is any advice I can give to new admission counselor (or anyone in a sales-oriented profession for that matter) is to always give great customer service. Doing something above and beyond the call of duty makes a great lasting impression.

The most extreme example I can give happened when I was working for Wartburg in the late 70's. I was young and foolish, so when a blizzard was predicted, I did not even think twice about driving from Waverly, IA to Iowa City, IA in the blizzard (20 inches of snow). There was a student with very high grades and test scores who was our top prospect...and I was bound and determined to recruit him. As I drove, I realized I was really the only car out on the road. I think I stayed on the road most of the time...It was a little more like driving a snowmobile than driving a car (now that I reflect back on it). I finally arrived at my hotel which was about a mile from this student's home. I had made an appointment to do a "home visit" with him and his parents. After checking in to the hotel and getting my luggage squared away, I walked out to my car only to find that it was completely blocked in by a giant snowbank. Hmmm. I opened the back hatch of my car (a Pacer!--- It was a little bit like driving a flying saucer)

and pulled out my cross-country skis. I was an avid cross-country skier at that time in my life. I strapped on the skis, grabbed my poles, and cross country skied the entire mile to the student's home.

Icicles hanging from my beard, he answered the door and said "wow...you must really want me!" Unfortunately, he ended up going to Luther College (Wartburg's greatest rival at the time)... so not all recruiting stories have happy endings...but I certainly gave it my all!

Kate B was a student from Dundee Crown HS who came to visit campus with her dad, Chet. Kate really wanted to do the walking tour of campus, but she had recently sprained her ankle, so she was on crutches. I will never forget the sad look on her face when she realized she couldn't keep up with the group. So Chet and I put her in my car...and I drove from building to building... helping her out of the car at every building so she could see it. Every time I see her (she is now an art teacher at her old high school) we laugh about her campus tour. Every time we re-tell the story it gets grander and grander ("I carried her on my shoulders"...etc.), but the important thing is that she got to see our beautiful campus and she is now a proud alum.

On a Friday night, after a hard work-week...every young admission rep has only one thing on their mind: beer. Maybe two things: beer and pizza. Anything to relax. When I was a rookie admission rep (in 1977), on Fridays we would leave the office pretty much at exactly 5:00. Other days, we were there until 8 or 9 at night, but Fridays, we tried to get out earlier.

On one particular Friday night...I was the last one out of the office (about 5:15 or so...). I had one foot in my car when a car pulled up with Illinois license plates. Not too many people who visit Waverly, IA have Illinois plates (at least not in 1977). I could have just put my other foot in the car and driven away... but something (that damn German work ethic of mine) in me told me to speak with the two young men who were in the car from Illinois.

Jimmy S and Paul G were the visitors from Illinois. Both were 18 year old young men who were out on a quest (without their parents) to find their collegiate home.

It turns out they we both not only good students, but excellent athletes as well. Jimmy was a basketball player...Paul was a baseball pitcher. I introduced myself to them and led them back up the steps to the admission office. Eventually, the basketball and baseball coaches came in and the five of us talked until after 9 o'clock. So much for my relaxing evening of pizza and beer.

Over the years, I had the pleasure of developing a close relationship with both boys, and even though I had left Wartburg by then, I went back to their graduation. I remember talking with Paul in his room prior to graduation. He was very emotional about leaving his Wartburg home, so I did my best to calm him. There is no crying in baseball...but there certainly was that day in his dorm room...

Jimmy eventually became an admission counselor...then a basketball coach (I went to visit him and his wife in Texas where he coached). Paul (or "Groto" as we lovingly called him) played professional baseball in Europe, then eventually became a collegiate baseball coach in the suburbs of Chicago.

If I had just gotten into my car and driven away that night...who knows? Sometimes the simplest effort gets the best results. Knowing Jimmy and Groto has been much more rewarding than going home to eat pizza and drink beer. Admission representatives always have to think "long term gratification" over "short term gratification."

Back in the day (Now I am starting to sound like my grandfather. Sorry.) the one way to really go "above and beyond" was to visit with students in their homes. I no longer do this. Now, I meet with families at Starbucks (partially because it is a neutral location where parents do not have to feel like they have to feed or entertain me, and partly because I have an unhealthy addiction to ice-venti-mocha-nonfat-decaf-extra-ice-double-cup drinks. Truly. I need therapy.)

The stories I can tell about home visits are many. The most horrifying occurred when I made an appointment with a young lady at her parents' apartment. She told me that here parents are "always home by 4pm."

I knocked on the door at 4:00 and when she opened the door there was a cold beer on the table, soft music in the background, and no parents. I ran SO quickly away from there to a pay phone (again, Google it. We used to use pay phones back in prehistoric times) to call my boss.

"You won't believe what just happened to me!" Needless to say, this student never ended up coming to my college! Thank goodness.

One home visit ended up in a Canasta card game that lasted well past midnight (they needed a fourth...so who was I to say no?).

Luke was my best buddy by my second visit to another student's home. He liked to sit on my lap and lick my face. Luke was a 7 foot tall (on his hind legs) Great Dane with a heart of gold. He really was drawn to me for some reason, so when I would try to leave the house after talking with the family, he would jump on my shoulders and virtually knock me to the floor. I miss Luke. I did two or three visits to this family. Mostly to see Luke I must admit.

F Gomez was a 16 year old young genius who had skipped at least a couple grades in school and was graduating from high school with straight A's and a very high ACT. He lived in a neighborhood in Chicago that was known for a lot of criminal activity. The day before I visited with him and his family in their one room apartment (family of 12...he was the oldest), a young child had been killed and stuffed in a garbage can close to his home. It was that kind of neighborhood. When I stepped in to his tiny apartment, I was shocked to see twelve mats neatly stacked in the corner. At night they would take those mats down to sleep on. The thought of F leaving to go to college 6 hours away in Iowa was very disturbing to the Mom. In his entire 16 years, he had never really been anywhere outside of Chicago, but he was bound and determined to go to Wartburg. It was a great home visit. I think I learned more than he did, actually, but the home visit made the mom more comfortable with the thought of her oldest boy leaving home. He ended up graduating in only three years from Wartburg as a Social Work/Pre-Med student and is now a successful doctor.

Sometimes it is difficult to keep one's temper in check. Case in point: a home visit to the daughter of a V.P. for a major agricultural organization. The parents were quite wealthy and the home was spectacular. When I mentioned the cost of our college, the dad told me that "girls don't really need college. They can just get married and be a housewife." He refused to pay for her education even though he obviously could afford it. Tears in the girls eyes. I left. So sad.

One other way to go "above and beyond" are what we call "Activity Visits." If the student is a musician...go to their concert. If the student is a thespian...go to their theatre production. If the student is an athlete...go watch them complete. I have probably seen 6 productions of Oliver, 3 of Joseph and the Amazing Multicolored Dreamcoat, and countless productions of The Sound of Music. I have stood in the rain watching students play soccer, shivered in the dark watching football players, and been hit by many a volleyball that was hit the wrong direction.

I get very few speeding tickets (considering that I drive 15,000 or more miles a year, this is a good thing), however, one dark and rainy evening I was driving to see Carolyn M in a production of Nunsense. The speed limit dropped (without warning) from 55 to 30 in what I am sure is the most active speed trap on Route 47 in northern Illinois. "I am going to give you a ticket" is all the officer had to say. Okey dokey. The musical was awesome, Carolyn was a star, and she ended up coming to my college and graduating with honors. The sacrifices I make!

Caitlin W is now an evening news anchor for a TV station in the Midwest and still keeps in touch with me. I remember (just like it was yesterday) going to see her play Liesl in the Sound of Music. It is also so much fun to watch one of my own recruits on TV.

Jennifer D played the main character in a high school production of Meet Me in Saint Louis. When Monmouth put on this same play just recently, I emailed Jennifer to ask her if she was going to do a guest (alum) performance for us. She replied that her voice probably isn't what it used to be.

Annie was one of the main characters in a production of Little Shop of Horrors. Personally, I think her high school performance was better than some professional productions I have seen. While at Monmouth, she traveled to Italy and was able to learn opera.

One time I went to see a young man play basketball. His coach heard that I was coming, and he did not want him to go to my college, so he benched the kid for the entire game. The student was so embarrassed.

Yes, these "activity visits" help me recruit the students, but I believe I "receive more than I give." It is so heartwarming to watch these kids progress through college, graduate, and go on to have families and successful careers. Thank goodness for Facebook. I am on Facebook with over 400 of my recruits, so every day I learn something new about all the lives that I have touched over the years. I have even had an opportunity to attend several weddings of my recruits. One of the most memorable was Joe K's wedding. Joe and his wife are Polish. The service was in Polish and every both at the church service and at the reception were Polish. Have you ever been to a Polish reception? It went on for over two days. My wife and I couldn't make it past about the three-hour mark. No clue what anyone said, but we had an awesome time nonetheless.

One day I had two weddings to go to in the same day (in towns 2 hours apart) so I went to the wedding (but not the reception) for wedding #1 (which was a bagpipe wedding because both the bride and groom played bagpipes for us at Monmouth)...then drove like crazy to get to the reception (but not ceremony) for wedding #2. I still keep in touch with these "kids". No matter how old they get...they are still kids to me.

CHAPTER 18---IT ALL BEGAN WITH A CUP OF COFFEE

I was born in Clinton Iowa on June 27, 1952. I inherited my "damn German work ethic" from my dad, Jim Pitts. I seldom saw my dad as I was growing up...he worked about 70 hours a week as the owner/manager of Marcucci's Restaurant (best coffee, candy, ice cream in the world; the rest of the menu not so good LOL).

(my dad is on the left in this picture)

My mom helped him from time to time at the cash register. Clinton is a little town of about 20,000 people...and over half of them knew my dad by name. Everywhere I would go in Clinton, as I was growing up, people would call me Jim. I viewed it as a compliment, so I never really corrected them.

Names.

Can't do them. Cannot do instant-recall of a name. Just doesn't happen.

My dad couldn't do them...and I am afraid I inherited that from him too. Everyone knew his name, but even if my dad knew someone for 30 years, he quite often couldn't remember their name.

I have heard that is an actual diagnosable "learning disability," but all I know is that it is frustrating.

Every year I worked with about 1500 prospective students. About 250 of them applied for admission, and sometimes only 20-80 of them enrolled. Names and faces swirl around in my head. I just cannot do them. The worst for me is when a room has prospective students (still in high school), current Monmouth students, and Monmouth alums all at the same time. It's like my brain explodes. Who is who? What is that name...it's on the tip of my tongue...HELP!!!! Then, about ten minutes after a student leaves the room it hits me...their name! Too late...but at least I remembered. Often I can remember everything about them (except for the name). An even harder puzzle for me to figure out is the parents. When they get separated from their son or daughter at one of our programs, remember who is the parent of who makes my brain explode!

One time, one of my recruits (who was working in our food service department) came up to me and said "What's my name?" I froze. Could not think of it. She viewed this as my not caring about her as a person and treated me very coolly. She was hurt. Since then, we have met several times and I DO now remember her name. She and I get along really well now. I hate this little "chink in my armor" but I have learned to compensate.

My dad and I are a LOT alike, both of us with that name-memory-thing...and that damn German work ethic!

Work ethic is the key to my profession, but "people skills" are crucial as well. I learned this early on, at age 11, as a paperboy for the Clinton Herald Newspaper Company. I didn't just deliver the paper, I became friends with my customers and, at times, was just that "someone" for the elderly (and alone) folks that just wanted/needed someone to talk to. I think that I knew, deep down inside, that I was doing more than just earning money delivering papers. This prepared me well for my Admission career. Sometimes, especially when parents are upset about something, all they really want is someone who will "be there for them" and just listen and empathize with them.

Then, when I turned 16, I continued to work for the Clinton Herald as an early morning and late day switchboard operator. This is where my people skills were sharpened. Calming people down when they called to say that they didn't get their paper (or that the Clinton Herald driver threw the paper out the truck window and hit them in the butt with it...true story...or when our driver, on accident, hit and killed a farmer's prize hog) taught me how to deal with the public, handle objections, and try to remain tactful and kind even when the temptation was to scream or laugh.

I also had the pleasure of working in a factory for two summers. I think everyone should have to do hard labor like this at some point in their life. Working side by side with hard-working blue collar laborers was an experience I will never forget. I ended up in the best physical shape of my life...but more than anything it taught me that I really wanted and needed a college education so I wouldn't have to spend my whole life doing manual labor. It was a cardboard carton factory where they printed all the cardboard cartons that packaged food comes in. The printed on large sheets, perforated them, and stacked them about 1000 high. I then had to take an air-hammer with a chisel tip and strip out the stacks of boxes. My title: "Stripper." Try putting THAT on your resume!

I went to Mount Saint Clare College (no longer in operation which saddens me greatly) for my first two years of college, then Wartburg for my B.A. (in Sociology---or as I like to call it "people studies"), and finally, the University of Iowa for my M.A. (in Sociology). Getting a Master's degree is really important for anyone thinking about a career in Admissions. It is almost impossible to climb the Admission ladder to leadership positions without a Masters.

Now to the coffee story...

About 6 months prior to receiving my Masters, I was unemployed and living in Waverly, IA (where Wartburg College is). Every day I would sit and have coffee with college administrators, professors, and other staff members who I knew from my undergraduate days.

On day, the College President and I were drinking our coffee when he said: "We have a job in Admissions. Are you interested in the position?" "What is Admissions?" I asked? Seriously... even though I went through the process myself three times at three different institutions, I didn't really know what an Admissions job entailed. The President just smiled and said "Don't worry. You will like it." And that was it. No interview. No resume. Just: Here is your job!

Looking back, I should have known the impact that a College Admission Counselor has on a student. I had finished my first two years of college at Mount Saint Clare and had applied as a transfer student to Loras, Coe, and Monmouth. I was debating between Math (which was my major at Mount Saint Clare) and Sociology (which was a subject I was just beginning to fall in love with). In fact, there is an area of study called Mathematical Sociology which is something I was interested in exploring. I told this to my Admission Rep from Wartburg, Jack Fistler. A week later, while mowing my lawn (shirtless and sweaty) I heard the beep of a car horn. It was Jack Fistler. He had gone to the Wartburg Library and checked out a copy of a "Mathematical Sociology" book. Wow. He truly went that extra mile! I was so impressed that Loras and Coe disappeared from my radar and I ended up at Wartburg.

I still have my first letter of appointment.

January 7, 1977

Mr. V. Peter Pitts
Wartburg College
Waverly, Iowa 50677

Dear Mr. Pitts:

I am happy to confirm your appointment as an Admissions Counselor effective January 6, 1977. Your base salary will be at the annual rate of $8,500. Since our fringe benefit package is on the order of sixteen percent, the annual rate of total compensation would be approximately $9,860.

This appointment will be subject to review upon the appointment of a new director of admissions.

Welcome aboard. We are pleased to have you with us.

Sincerely,

Wow. $8500 (working about 60 hours a week). There was absolutely no training for me. My first day, I walked in the door... they handed me a briefcase, and told me my first appointment was at Independence High School at 10:00 and sent me out the door. Welcome to Admissions!

At first I didn't really like working in Admissions. I was nervous and very unsure of myself. Not knowing answers to questions really bothered me. My first visit with a family, in the Admissions Office, began with the dad's question: "How much is your endowment?" I froze. What the hell is an endowment???

I also almost got fired. Our numbers were low, so the college hired an Admissions consulting firm. That is never a good sign. Workers need to really keep on their toes to make sure the consultant does not recommend dismissal. Well, we were working at least 60 hours a week...a lot of evening hours and weekend hours (after all...to reach students by phone, the best time is 4-8 in the evening). So, as a stress release, the Admission reps would take an hour over their lunch break to go play tennis. The consultants noticed that we were not at our desks and recommended our dismissal. Thank goodness Drew Boster (one of my favorite Directors of all time) saved our butts. Thank you so much Drew! And Drew...I am so sorry about the 12 long-distance calls (these were costly back in the 70's) I made trying to recruit that one student from Alaska...who did not enroll, by the way.

Over time, however, the more I learned, the more I enjoyed what I did. In fact, after only three years as an Admission Rep, I applied for, and received a Director of Admission position at St. Francis in Fort Wayne Indiana (this one paid a whole $16,500 a year. I thought I was rich!). It turns out that life as a Director is not nearly as much fun as life as a recruiter. It certainly introduced me the wild and wacky world of college "internal politics." Faculty, Administration, Staff, Secretaries, Maintenance, Trustees, etc. each have their own agenda. A college admission director has to somehow juggle all these agendas while walking a tightrope that is burning from both ends. Every college president (with pressure from their Board of Trustees) wants more students each year, with higher academic credentials, bringing in more money, and still increase the ethnic diversity of the institution. This is a little like winning five trifectas in a row at the racetrack after having won the lottery two weeks in a row. It just doesn't happen. But year after year we try. Does Wile E Coyote ever catch the fox? Does Charlie Brown ever actually get to kick the football? Does Gilligan ever get off the island? That is the life of an Admission Director.

After three years as a Director, I went back to Wartburg in my first venture as a Regional Director. Working from my home was great, but Wartburg never truly committed to the "regional" role (I had to go to campus way too often, drive to southern Illinois way too often, etc.). I was never able to truly focus on JUST the Chicago area. Luckily, my former director at Wartburg accepted a position at Monmouth, so he asked me to join him. Thus began a life-long relationship with the greatest group of people I have ever known.

I did leave Monmouth once (to pursue a Directorship again...at two different places in Missouri), but I soon came to my senses and went back to my regional position with Monmouth. President Bruce Haywood saved my life by bringing me back with Monmouth. A lot of colleges would not have given someone a second chance, but Bruce did...and every time I saw him (sadly, he passed away in 2020) I thanked him over and over again! I was with Monmouth over 27 years until my retirement (May 12, 2019).

CHAPTER 19---MY ADMISSION LIFE IN 3 PICTURES

<u>Age 2 (learning how to make calls to prospective students)</u>

<u>Age 31 Working for Monmouth in Chicagoland</u>

Age 60-something...soon to retire (see the happy look on my face)

CHAPTER 20---THE "DIRECTOR YEARS"

In retrospect, I really don't know what the hell I was thinking. I was Director of Admission at three different institutions (one in Indiana and two in Missouri). In fact, one of these three was actually an Assistant Vice President position. I was an "ok" Director/AVP...but not exactly a great one. I think I did this mostly because it was the "expected progression" in the Admission profession (and the money of course.) One was supposed to go from counselor, to Assistant Director, to Associate Director, to Director, etc.. In the end...I pretty much was the perfect example of what many call the "Peter Principal" (people keep getting promoted until they get to their level of incompetence), however it was so much "incompetence" as it was "incongruousness." It just wasn't the right "fit" for me. Just like students need to have the right fit in a college, those of us in the work force need to find the right fit in regard to our employment.

Dealing with staffing, budgets, campus politics, hiring/firing, denying students, and other aspects of being a director really wore me down. There were some fun parts of it. For example, being able to sit at what I call the "big decisions table" with the President and Vice Presidents for their weekly meeting was awesome. Seeing how decisions are made takes some of the mystery away from things. Directors end up knowing things that they really cannot talk with employees about---things that they hear their employees endlessly complaining about---until a certain point in time when it is "ok" to talk about it. I really enjoyed "big picture stuff." Planning for the future. What names of prospective students should we buy? What recruiting brochures should we publish? What photos and text should go into these brochures? I also really enjoyed the statistical aspect of things. My nickname from a lot of my employees (at the least the ones that were not used behind my back) was "stat man." To this very day, as a retired Regional Director, I really enjoy crunching numbers, long range planning, etc.. I have a routine and a strong work ethic even though there is nothing really that I need to do.

Another aspect of being a Director that I really enjoyed was hiring, training, and mentoring new admission counselors. In one of my Director positions (in Missouri), I inherited an empty office. I had to hire a whole new group of secretaries and admission representatives. This turned out to be absolutely the most awesome, tight-knit group of co-workers I have ever had the pleasure of working with. We all seemed to think the same thoughts, finish each other's sentences, and totally function as a very self-less and well-oiled machine. I miss those people greatly.

Lots of crazy/bizarre/sad things occurred during my Director years. One of my counselors at my first directorship (in Indiana), Keith (who was even more of a workaholic than me), was a diabetic who did not do what the doctor told him...and ended up paying the ultimate price. I was sitting in a hotel room in St. Louis overlooking The Arch, when my phone rang. It was my counselor's brother calling to tell me that Keith had died that evening. That next week, at a very sad funeral, I was one of the people who eulogized him. Very tough to get through that speech. I think of Keith often.

At another college I had to deal with a coach (who for some reason was supposed to turn in his mileage when he went out recruiting to me for approval) who fudged his expense report by over $200. I refused to sign his expense report...so he met me at my office one day, closed the door, and told me he had "people" who could "take care of me." Hmmm. I opened the door, asked him to leave, and went to have a chat with the President and the head of Security.

Another employee broke into a locked filing cabinet and stole over $300 in cash. He then just "disappeared." Never came back to work. Turns out he had a police record that we didn't know of.

One employee made over $100 in long distance phone calls on the college phone to his girlfriend in California (this was back when there was such a thing as paying more for long distance phone calls). I brought this to his attention, and his resignation was on my desk the next day.

One of my receptionists had to be fired. She was actually being rude to guests. Over a half dozen reports from visitors about her rudeness led to the firing. She sued for unemployment comp---and won. Sigh.

Fun times as a Director. Not.

Needless to say, being a Regional Director (where all I really had to do is manage myself) was a welcome relief. So, basically, 32 of my 42 years in the profession I worked from home in the Chicago area, not from campus.

CHAPTER 21---THE PHYSICAL, PSYCHOLOGICAL, AND EMOTIONAL TOLL OF BEING A COLLEGE RECRUITER

It was the first time I had ever visited Noble Street Charter School (the original campus of this Nationally known and respected charter network). I had no idea which door to enter (it is in a rather nondescript building on the north side of Chicago), so I struck up a conversation with one of the maintenance men who was exiting the building. While we chatted, my hand was resting on the back fender of a Buick. Our conversation ended, and I entered the building, checked in at Security, and began walking up the steps. I heard a tremendous crash from outside, followed by screams and eventually police and ambulance sirens. I didn't think more about it (this is Chicago after all, right?) and met with the classroom of students who were eager to learn about Monmouth. After my presentation, I departed the building. Wow. There were literally two cars on top of one another. A Chevy was on top of the Buick exactly where my hand had been resting. It turns out I escaped death by about 25 seconds. My heart skipped a beat, yet I had to go on. There were more schools to visit that day.

Weather in Chicago is always kind of a crapshoot...I cannot tell you how many college fairs I have attended where a tornado touched down nearby. In fact, there was one at St. Charles North HS one year where all the admission counselors and students were told to leave the gym and go to the hallways because there was a tornado approaching. As I stood in the hallway, one of the counselors at the high school whispered to me that he knew where all the food was...so we slipped away into the kitchen to munch. We figured if we were going to die, we might as well die happy and well-fed.

Another time, after leaving the St. Patrick college night program, the rain was coming down SO hard and so quickly, that my car actually started to float. Float. Like a boat. My heart was beating SO fast! Once it sank so that tires were touching the ground, I drove quickly but carefully to the nearest hotel. Even though I was only a few minutes from my suburban home, I wasn't going to take any more chances. I slept in my clothes and went home the next day to take a shower.

When I was at Wartburg, I had to make "x" number of calls every day...so even though we were experiencing a major thunder and lightning storm, I persevered and made my calls. Lightning hit not even 4 feet away from my window...completely splitting (like a corkscrew) a tree whose branches were touching my window. The tree was smoking. I decided not to make my quota of calls that night.

At least three times, my drive to the Monmouth campus involved very rough weather. One time I just missed a tornado by about 15 minutes. I hid in a cooler of a convenience store until it passed.

Physical and mental exhaustion is common when doing large open house or scholarship programs. We are responsible for SO many people (especially when we bus them in from Chicago... we have the extra responsibility of the lives of 50+ people per bus). Plus we have to be "on" at all times and attend to the needs of every single student. One night, after one of these programs. I laid down on my bed in the local hotel to watch TV (to relax) and woke up the next morning with my suit, tie, and even nametag still on. TV still going. I had slept over 12 hours.

Pulling a catalog case filled with brochures, standing for hours at a time in one place behind a table at a college fair, leaning over the table to talk to students, and having to talk at a loud decibel just to be heard (in a loud college fair setting) have caused all sorts of physical issues. My shoulders are hunched over...my back will never be healthy again, my legs and feet have several "issues", I ended up with a DVT (blood clot) from standing and sitting in place all the time, and I have developed a vocal condition called Spasmodic Dysphonia. Again, Google it...but basically my vocal chords kind of have a mind of their own...certain words just cannot come out...the voice sounds raspy and strained. In fact (and thank goodness this happened when kids would rather text than talk) I cannot make phone calls anymore. In doing some research, I have found that lots of people who use their voice a LOT for a living (radio celebrities, politicians, etc.) tend to get this, usually after the age of 50. I remember where I was the first day my voice decided not to work. It was at an ACM (Associated Colleges of the Midwest) college fair and panel. I was a speaker on the panel, and this dysphonia began about half-way through my presentation.

I went to a Spasmodic Dysphonia specialist who confirmed that yes, I do have S.D.. The treatment is botox injections in the vocal chords. Big long needles. Not fun. Anyway, I said "go ahead." Well...I ended up talking like Mickey Mouse or Mister Moose (from Captain Kangaroo)

for 7 weeks. I even had to give a classroom presentation to a group of kids when I was talking that way. I apologized to the kids in my high squeaky voice and told them to go home and do a YouTube search for Mister Moose. One student actually did this and emailed me that (LOL) yes, I did sound just like Mister Moose. I have given up on the Botox fix and have decided to just "deal with it."

Luckily the college understood my disability and hired Iris S (part time) to make calls to students for me. Iris S is a retired high school counselor. I have known her for years! She is bilingual (I am not) so it was really handy having her talk with the Latinx families, especially about financial aid. Here is a great pick of her from her Facebook page: (she is the one on the right)

My own communication with students needs to be in person (once I get talking for a while, it is easier to speak. It is beginning that is the difficulty), by text, by email, or via any other form of social media. I think I am still as effective---but it is frustrating. What I enjoy the most, ironically, is a "classroom presentation" because talking for a long time is easier than talking in short spurts. Plus, if there is a white-board and set of markers to work with, I can write something out that is impossible or difficult to articulate. I wish I had a portable white board with me every-where I go!

CHAPTER 22---IT'S HELL TO GET OLD

As a young admission representative at the age of 25, no-one called me "Mr. Pitts"...or (even worse) "Sir." Students called me Peter. I cannot remember the exact time and place, but at some point that all changed. With a last name like "Pitts," the last think I want to be called is "Mr. Pitts," but now (at the tender age of 60-something) I have resigned myself to that moniker. When I am recruiting in the inner-city especially...a lot of kids will call me "Mr. Peter." Someone tells me this is a "Southern" thing...but, really, just so you don't call me late for dinner, you can call me anything!

Relating to students is different now too. From age 25-35, students viewed me as a "young/hip/friend." From age 35-55, they viewed me as a parent-or-teacher-figure of sorts. Now, as my AARP and Medicare memberships make my wallet fatter...they view me as that "grandfatherly one who is helping them with their future." Sage wisdom, right?

Socializing changes too. In my 20's and even in my 30's, it was always fun to go out with other admission reps after a college fair for a drink or two. As I grew older and had children this stopped completely. I just let the young'uns destroy their brain cells while I got to bed at a "sensible time." No more burning the candle at both ends for me!

CHAPTER 23---EVOLUTION OF THE ADMISSION PROFESSION

I have seen a LOT of changes in the 42+ years I was in the Admission profession.

Computerization. In 1977, we had a physical "card" for each recruit. We kept the cards in metal box with indexes for each high school. We wrote notes on the cards and filed them away. When we went to visit a high school, we would actually take the batch of cards out, rubber band them, and carry them with us to the schools. Now, we have a sophisticated computer system (CRM) that allows us a lot more flexibility and gives us a million different ways to organize our data. I do miss the cards, though. There is something about seeing actual handwriting that tells a lot about the student that a computer printout just cannot match.

Competition. In the Chicago area especially, the competition for students is fierce. One indicator of this is the growth of the organization called C.A.R.R. (Chicago Area Regional Representatives) of which Monmouth is a member. In 2000, there were only about a dozen colleges that had regional reps in the Chicago area. Now there are 125 reps from close to 100 different colleges who have regional reps. In 2000, a "big" college fair would have 30 to 40 colleges in attendance. Now, there are some huge college fairs with over 300 colleges in attendance. In the 70's and 80's, students would apply to about a half dozen colleges at most. Now it is not unusual for kids to apply to as many as 15 to 20 colleges. Competition for students is more intense than ever. I really feel sorry for the students who feel the results of this. I cannot imagine the daily number of emails and social media messages that these students receive. It has become, also, quite a "bidding war" with financial aid. Some colleges, who are desperate to survive or who are desperately in need of a certain demographic, are offer tremendous financial incentives to students. Because of this, colleges keep increasing their costs (so they can fund the scholarships they are offering). Crazy. The actual cost is a LOT less than the "sticker price," especially at small private colleges that do not have a huge National following.

Communication. In the 1970's and 80's, our correspondence with students was mostly by telephone. We also did a lot with handwritten notes. In the 70's and 80's, students might get a couple brochures in the mail from the colleges, but that was about it...until they applied...and then they would get a few more letters. Now, however, most colleges have a whole set of very specialized brochures that they send, coupled with a whole series of very targeted letters and HTML emails. They put targeted ads embedded in social media sites. Very few admission reps write handwritten notes (the sad thing is that many kids do not know how to read cursive because they were never taught cursive). Texting and use of social media has totally changed the way we communicate with students and their families. Given my voice issues this has been a real blessing for me.

The Application Process. In the late 90's, every college had printed (paper) applications that students would complete with an ink pen and mail to the college. Transcripts and test score would then be printed on paper and sent to the campus as well. Now everything is electronic. With the Common App, for example, a student can type their name, address, etc. only once...and then send it to a number of different colleges all with the click of their mouse. This makes it easy for students to apply to 20+ colleges. Most colleges no longer have paper application forms. Most only have students apply online. Then, to review the file to decide if a student is admitted, we no longer have a paper physical file...we can do it all on our computer. More and more colleges have no application fee and/or are "test optional" (meaning that the student does not have to submit ACT/SAT scores to be considered for admission).

Meeting with students. Visits to high schools were more productive in the 70's and 80's than they are today. Since there were fewer colleges visiting high schools, teachers were a little more receptive to allowing students to miss a class (or a portion of a class) to meet with us. Now, with more colleges competing for students, with more rigid academic requirements evolving in high schools, and with uber-competitive programs like International Baccalaureate expanding, teachers are less willing to allow students to miss class time to visit with us. College fairs have so many colleges in attendance, that the amount of time a student can spend with any one rep is diminished. Basically, face to face time with admission reps is the least I have ever seen in my 42 years in the profession. With the proliferation of social media, it is getting increasingly difficult to "get the attention" of the students face to face, so now we are in a cyber battle with other colleges to get their attention. I suspect that all this cyber communication becomes nothing but a blur for the students.

As I am writing these words, we are in the midst of the Covid19 Pandemic, which means that the entire search, visit, admission and financial aid cycle is being done virtually via Zoom. This will likely change the entire admission process in the future. Time will tell.

CHAPTER 24---
FARMER B.O.B.

Admissions is a lot like farming. Farmers plant their seeds in the springtime. Throughout the summer, they watch the plants grow. Farmers never really know if they are going to have a bumper crop or if they are going to lose everything. Working 16 hour days, they need to till, plant, fertilize, and kill the weeds. Then they need Mother Nature to provide water (but not too much water). Then, in the fall, they need to harvest their crop, take it in to be sold, and start counting their return on investment. In the winter, they need to clean their equipment, do planning for the next year, and rest a bit...because before they can blink an eye, it will once again be time to do it all over again!

One of the best admission counselors I have ever worked with was Sherm F. He was from a really small town in western Iowa (less than 700 people in his entire town). It was, by most standards, a town "in the middle of nowhere." It was more than an hour to a grocery store, bank, or doctor. This little town's economy was 100% farm-driven. Sherm grew up on a farm...so he truly understood the entire process of crop production and agricultural business management.

Becoming a college admission representative was, according to Sherm, "a piece of cake." He took to the profession (in his words) "like a duck takes to water". Sherm had a photographic memory. Not only did he remember his student recruits' names, but he knew their parents' names, their dogs' names, and everything else that you could imagine. I was SO envious of this ability. It really helped him in establishing close bonds with his recruits. He used to do a lot of "home visits" on farms. He always kept a pair of overalls in the trunk of his car. When it came time for the financial aid portion of the conversation, he would literally go out to the barn and talk money while helping the dad throw around bales of hay. Now THAT is going an extra mile.

It was Sherm that taught me the parallels between being a farmer and being a college recruiter.

In the fall, we plant the seeds. In other words, we go to various high schools, college fairs, and agencies gathering names of interested students. Then we weed and fertilize (send out follow-up mailings, invite students to scholarship competitions, encourage students to attend our open houses, etc.). We watch our crop (application numbers) grow. Application for admission numbers begin small (in August) and then grown to huge number by October and November. Then comes the financial aid process. Without financial aid (which is our "rain water"), our entire crop withers and dies. Too much financial aid--the college goes broke and closes. Unfortunately, nobody really wants to pay the entire cost of a college anymore.

In the spring and summer, we begin our harvest. The number of student who will eventually enroll is a bit of a crapshoot. We never really know until August exactly how many students we get. Then the process begins all over again.

The summer is a "farmer's winter." It is our time for planning, for evaluating, and resting just a bit. Before you know it, it will be September again, and time for us to put in our 16 hour days. An endless process---Ground Hog Day!!!

In the end...in both professions...in terms of the end product (the numbers in the end), you "get what you get." College presidents hate to hear me say that, but it is so true.

If you ask a farmer, in late winter as they begin to plan to plant their seeds, how much money they will make that year... the only answer that they can give is "it depends." There is no way to accurately predict that number. Will they have enough to take a vacation that next winter? Maybe. Will they have enough to build another addition onto their house or to buy another piece of equipment? Perhaps. Will they have enough to at least eat and care for their family. Hopefully. Farm families deal with <u>nothing but uncertainty</u> for a LONG period of time each year (year after year), yet there are farm families that have done this for generations.

When a college president asks us how many students we will bring in each year, the only true answer early in the recruitment season is: "well, our goal is _____, and we will do everything we can to reach that goal. From past years, x number of inquiries produced y number of applications that produced z number of new students." There is a little bit of science involved (consultants will tell you that there is a LOT of science involved--- that is how they make their money), but there is also a lot of "art" and a splash of "luck." As it gets closer to the beginning of the school's year, the number starts to gets a little more clear, but we never know. We are totally at the mercy of the whims of 18-year-old kids and their parents. I always tell people that the only number that counts is the "B.O.B." count...the "butts on the beds" number two weeks after classes start, and by this time we are already several months into the recruitment of the next class.

One year, I had a territory that produced a LOT of students. A territory that usually produced about 60 students was producing close to 100. This was the year that Kevin R (who invented/created our Big Red

Mascot) was dressed as Big Red, and was being introduced as an "incoming freshman." Our president at the time, told me that if I hit 100 recruits, he would cut off his tie at our "beginning of the year Matriculation Ceremony." I was at 99. Bummer, right? So imagine my surprise when the president announce that, since I had "recruited Big Red", that that brought me up to exactly 100. In front of hundred of people, he cut off his tie (people cheered and clapped) and gave it to me. Embarrassing, but totally cool and fun!

Note: "Big Red's" family made up really nice shirts that year with "Big Red's Mom," "Big Red's Dad," etc...for their whole family. Imagine my surprise and thrill when they presented me with my own t-shirt:

CHAPTER 25---OUR FAMILY AWAY FROM OUR FAMILY

Over the years, I have had the pleasure of working with some of the nicest, kindest, craziest people (both those in our office and the other reps we see "on the road.")

I will never forgive Larry from a competing small college for retiring before me. We are the same age, and have been in the profession for almost the exact same number of years. We always competed for students, yet have maintained a good friendship. I also said that when Larry left a college fair...we all had permission to leave. Technically, we are supposed to stay to the very end of a fair, but sometimes the number of students dwindle so much, that we (the Admission reps) outnumber the guests. Sometimes we are actually the only people left in the room. That is the time Larry would pack up. Now with him gone, no one will know when to leave! He will be missed. Watch for him on any local golf course. As a retirement gift I bought him a hat that says 50% IDK 50% IDC. It fits.

Em B was my hero. He has the all-time record (I think) for being a "road warrior"---43 years. He beat me by one year. He retired at the age of 72, but sadly passed away from cancer. He was one of the finest admission reps I have know. Kind, knowledgeable, responsive to the students. Whenever I had a question about a high school, or a guidance counselor, or anything pertaining to our profession, I would call upon him. He knew everyone! It seems like I could never arrive at a college fair before he did. If we were supposed to be there at 6, he was there at 5...waiting in his car, reading his newspaper. It seems like the older the rep, the earlier we show up for things. When Em retired, I assumed the mantle of "early arriver". It was a heavy cloak to wear, but every time I showed up early for a program early, I thought of him. The last time I saw him before he passed away was at Tasty Dog in Oak Park Illinois. We talked about his health prognosis and we reminisced about our many years together. He told me that, in retrospect, he wished that he had retired sooner, but he loved his job so much he really did not know what he would do without it. It probably wasn't even a year after he retired that he passed. I owe a lot to him. He will be missed for sure.

Ron T retired in 2014. He was the rep for Michigan State University. Every article of clothing I have ever seen him wear is Spartan Green. For a rep from a major university (whose table was totally swarmed immediately when the doors opened at a college fair), he took great personal interest in each and every student he spoke to. He knew EVERYTHING about Michigan State. He was continually re-educating himself about new programs on campus. He is one of those rare individuals (from a huge state university) who took phone calls, at home, from students at all hours of the day and night, including weekends and holidays. He gave the kind of personalized attention that you would expect from only a small college (where they do not have the huge quantity of students to work with). He is now retired, but I still saw him from time to time helping out at a sprinkling of college fairs. As I type this, he is asking me to be a "friend" on Facebook with him. YES. Of course. Truly a dedicated and hard-working professional. We need to do coffee soon!

There are about 100 more individuals I could list in this section, but let me shift my focus for a moment to some of the individuals who have worked with me at Monmouth.

Patty was our receptionist, our mother, our EVERYTHING in the office for many, many years. My favorite story to tell about her revolves around a telephone conversation we were having. Our boss at the time, Dick V (who I will write about in this chapter), was trying to get her attention...at the same time she was talking with me on the phone. She got flustered (because two conversations at the same time can be maddening, right?). I heard her say..."I have Peter in one Ear..." so I quickly shot back with "and Dick in the other, right?" She laughed so hard I think someone had to pick her up off the floor. Years later I bumped in to her in Galesburg. She didn't even say hi, she just said: "Peter in one ear." And I replied "and Dick in the other." Then we laughed and gave each other a big ol' bear hug. She was the glue that held our office together. I truly miss working with her.

Dick V is probably (no offense to all the other bosses I had over the years) one of the best supervisors/bosses I have had the pleasure to work with. He was the Director of Admission at the time that we grew from 480 students (heck, everyone had single rooms!) to over 1200 students ("WHAT? I have to have a room-mate????"). I call these the "Camelot Years" at Monmouth. During the years Dick was Director, and Dick Giese was President, we raised millions of dollars and constructed new dorms, a new sports complex, and increased the endowment.

Here is a picture of the awesome Admission staff we had during the "Camelot Years" (Dick is in the back row, second from the right):

Dick V was always "Mr. Cool Calm and Collected." Nothing really seemed to truly bother him unless he heard someone say "you don't have to sweat the small stuff." Those were fighting words for Dick. His insistence on "sweating the small stuff" is what made for the consistent growth in our enrollment. One day there was a tornado that moved through town and grazed the campus. Dick was up in his office, ignoring the tornado siren. Eventually, he went to the basement. When someone asked him why he finally succumbed to moving to the basement he said "well...a tree just flew by my window...so I figured it was time..." That is Dick for you. Cool and calm. When I retired, Dick had already retired from being President of another small college. I asked him for advice. He said to "stay busy and make a list of things to do each day. Treat it like a job." Great advice. That is exactly what I do.

Monmouth is a quiet little town. A lot of people don't even lock their doors at night. Dick lived in a beautiful house about half-way between downtown (where all the eating and drinking establishments are) and our campus. Dick (who, at this time, had been promoted to a Vice President position) and his wife seldom locked their front door. So...one night...one of our students got "over-served" at a local watering hole... When she wandered back to campus, she mistook his front door for the front door of her residence hall. Those doors are several blocks apart and look nothing like each other, but her mind was a bit fuzzy I guess.

When Dick woke up the next day, he walked downstairs to make the coffee and saw a girl sleeping on his beautiful antique couch. She had gotten sick on the couch (not good) and passed out.

Dick woke her up, explained to her that she was not in her dorm, asked for her parents' info (so he could get reimbursed for the couch), told her that he was Vice President of Monmouth, and then drove her back to her dorm. That girl spent some quality time in the Dean's office the next day. Note: Dick and his wife started locking their door after that.

Staff members at the time I retired ranged from newly hired reps...to individuals I worked with for more than 20 years. Dana, Michelle, Jayne, Chris (who I actually recruited to work for us), Kristi....too many to mention individually, but all of these became such good friends!!! I will keep in touch with them for sure.

Faculty members usually do not spend a lot of time in the admission office or helping with admission functions. There are exceptions (Monmouth has several faculty who are very involved), but one faculty member, "Doc" Kieft (who I spoke about earlier in this book) was one of those super-humans who did everything, knew everyone, and got very involved in helping us recruit students. He was at Monmouth for 33 years and was one of my best friends on campus. He passed away from cancer about 9 months after he retired.

I thought that what I learned from both Em Buie and Doc Kieft is that the secret to immortality is to NEVER retire...until I retired. And, so far, I am still breathing.

Rest in peace, Doc and Em.

CHAPTER 26---WATCHING MY "KIDS" GROW UP

Kids grow up. That is what they are supposed to do. They graduate from high school, graduate from college, spread their wings...and fly! I am continually amazed by the accomplishments of my 1500+ children. Note: people change jobs...so the following jobs were at least accurate at the time I wrote this.

Patrick is now the Principal of a Chicago elementary school. It seems like just yesterday I visited with him at his high school when he was a senior. Prior to switching to the elementary side, when he was principal at a charter high school, I enjoyed my many chats with him during my visits to that school.

Brad is a partner in one of Chicago's top law firms.

Dan is the owner of an errand-delivery system in the western suburbs of Chicago.

Mike Forkan is a lawyer in the suburbs of Chicago.

Danny is a lawyer in the State Capital of Illinois.

Tony (mentioned earlier in this book) owns his own film studio and produces horror films.

Jennifer is an Assistant Principal at a middle school close to my home. I remember meeting with her at her high school on Halloween one year when all the kids were dressed in outfits for Halloween (some of which were not exactly appropriate for prime time viewing...like the kid---not Jennifer---who was dressed as an anatomically correct cow...and another as an anatomically correct pig). She played soccer for us.

Katie is also a principal (so many alums of Monmouth are in leadership positions!). She is principal of an elementary school in the western suburbs of Chicago. I remember clearly how very homesick she was when she first arrived at Monmouth. Her mother and I almost had to tie her to her bed to keep her from leaving to go home. She tells me that her homesickness lasted pretty much her entire freshman year until her close friendships with fellow students finally convinced her to stay.

Juan (not his real name) is now an assistant superintendent for an entire Chicago suburban school system. His name is actually Andrew, but when he arrived on campus at Monmouth I asked him if he preferred to be called Andy or Andrew. He replied…"I don't care. You can call me Juan if you want to!" The nickname stuck. When I called his office one day a couple years ago to schedule lunch with him, his secretary was totally befuddled when I told her to "tell Juan that Peter called." Juan taught for a while, then became an elementary school principal when he was still in his 20's. I think he might have been one of the youngest principals ever in the State of Illinois. Now he is one of the top administrators in the school district. Awesome!

One Chicago-suburban high school's "teacher of the year almost every year" is none other than my recruit, my buddy, Kevin. Kevin is a singer, a coach, an awesome teacher, but more than anything, he is one of those very charismatic individuals who ALWAYS puts the needs of others before those of himself. He gets his head shaved every year to raise money for St. Baldricks. He performs (piano and voice) to raise money for Autism Speaks. He has been one of our top volunteers to help in Admission Recruiting (he helped with college fairs).

The first time Kevin visited campus as a high school senior, he attended one of our women's basketball games. There was no one available to sing the National Anthem, so he stood up and volunteers. So awesome! (Later that night he did ask me to help him find the name and number of one of the women's basketball players...which I did NOT do. LOL) He is a crazy, lovable character who is much loved by his students. In 2013, he was invited to speak at our commencement to accept the Young Alumnus Award. I am so proud to say I was his recruiter.

Ed Wimp is only in his early 30's, but he is already accomplished more than most 50 year olds! Here is a quote from his website:

Ed Wimp is an attorney, speaker, author, artist-manager and musician. On this site, you will be able to stay updated on all new information. Feel free to navigate around the website and connect via all social media.

Ed Wimp is an attorney, speaker, author, artist manager, and musician from Orlando, Florida. He started his career in music as a musician, and began recording and touring as a musician himself before transitioning into the business side of music.

After graduating college, Ed began transitioning into the business side of the music industry when he was presented with an opportunity to travel as part of the road management staff for R&B legends Earth Wind & Fire. From there, he was able to travel and tour with hip-hop icon A$AP Rocky as he appeared in the Under the influence Tour with Wiz Khalifa. Ed Wimp is the author of the book Building Fans, Fame & Wealth: The 18 Revenue Streams of Music. He travels to high schools, colleges, and conferences teaching aspiring musicians how to have a profitable music career.

After extensive touring while working in the music industry, Ed Wimp earned a law degree and now practices law. Ed takes joy in the opportunity to help people in their times of need and is honored to be a member of the profession.

Ed Wimp is a Renaissance Man. He has had many unique and outstanding experiences in his young life. Extensive International travel has been a cornerstone for Ed, which has given him a global perspective on life. Ed has enjoyed and retained the friendships of people from many parts of the world.

Ed is an avid golfer and takes the opportunity to play whenever his busy schedule allows.

Ed's first book <u>Building Fans, Fame, and Wealth: the 18 revenue streams of music</u> has been well received and has met with rave reviews. Ed was on our campus a few years ago to give a presentation to our students about his secret to success. The world will hear a lot about this man in the future. One of my awesome recruits!!! So proud! I cannot believe he got a book published before me...

Tom Hill is one of my most unique (and I am saying that in the most complimentary fashion) recruits of all time. He is the founder and director of the Carnival of Curiosity and Chaos, which is a performance art company in Chicago. Here is info about Tom from his website:

Tom Hill first created the Carnival of Curiosity & Chaos out of his love for the freak show. Tom is a self- determined creator, dreamer, trickster, extremist, circus performer and escape artist. Driven by an incredible passion for self-expression and the arts he assembled this circus sideshow collective after being long eschewed by several venues. He has now performed all over the United States working with performance arts venues for over 15 years providing excellent and talented performance art.

When Tom was in high school, he put on a two-hour magic show for the public. I had the pleasure of attending that concert. At Monmouth I saw him walk on broken glass, swallow fire, hang from a trapeze upside down and escape from a straight-jacket, and other daring endeavors...but he also created ceramic masks, wrote and directed a play (I still have a signed copy of the program from his play...and I have my ticket stub as well), and basically just took over the campus.

In 2016, Tom brought his performance art troupe to our campus. To quote our campus newspaper:

As a Monmouth College student, Tom Hill '04 straddled the line between theatre and art.

Although Hill had opportunities to go down only one academic path, he is grateful that he took the broader approach at a liberal arts college. Both of his majors have become part of his highly successful performance art business, The Carnival of Curiosity and Chaos.

"I wanted to be able to do it all," said Hill of his choice to attend Monmouth and double-major in art and theatre.

Monmouth attracts many students with artistic and entrepreneurial aspirations, and I am so happy to say that Tom Hill is one of the best!

There are SO many other awesome stories of what my recruits are doing (professionally) after graduation. Recently (July 2020) I posted, to all my recruits on Facebook, the question: "Where are you now?" Here is an edited sampling of my their responses:

Andrew: Been with my dream job for 3 1/2 years now as a key account rep/sales for the best online music marketplace in the world!

Becky: I am an Instructional Math Coach in a school district! I LOVE it!

Janet: I went on to obtain a Masters of Education in School Counseling from Saint Xavier University. Soon after, I was hired as social worker and social emotional counselor at a charter high school in Chicago. And because of my experience as a dancer on MC's dance team, I was able to coach the dance team as well! I am currently a full time stay at home parent and home educator in Florida. I'm also very involved in my community.

Nikki: I got my MHRM (Masters in Human Resource Management) while working for a university as a Business Process Analyst for the National Registrar Services department. Just celebrated my 10 year anniversary with the organization!

Fannetta: I'm a high school English teacher and department head here in Chicago. Before coming back to Chicago, I taught in Galesburg, IL for five years.

Alexis: living in Suburbs of Chicago and am currently in my first year of my Doctorate of Physical Therapy Program

Lindsey: Received my Masters of Occupational Therapy in 2012. I work as an Occupational Therapist in a geriatric population

Devon: I am a practicing Veterinarian in Los Alamos, New Mexico

Becky: Living in the suburbs of Chicago and hit my 18-yr anniversary, this month, at a major bank as a Product Owner in Commercial Card.

Bridget: Living in Ohio. My full time job is sales and customer service for a racing lane line company. Only 3 companies in the world and ours is #1 for collegiate and upper level (Olympic) competitions. I meet some pretty unique people. Its fun! I also put my physical education degree into work and own my own little fitness studio.

Samantha: Stay at home mom to 2 boys. Enjoying life with our 2 Bengal cats.

Christopher: US Navy Veteran. Now, a private security instructor, EMT, and small arms instructor. Living in Las Vegas area. Currently working on my BSN.

Kimberly: I currently live just outside of Chicago. For the last 5 years I have worked for a restaurant and hospitality supply company. I started in the call center and currently work as a multi-unit coordinator for top performing sales reps.

Kelly: I am living in western IL and teaching high school history. I have been the union president for 10 of the last 14 years and I have served on the Illinois Education Association board of directors and their executive committee.

Becca: I'm (a librarian in the suburbs of Chicago) with (a) MLIS from Dominican University. I've been with my library for nearly 15 years, cataloging (my love) for nearly 20 years, and I am now also working part-time at an additional library.

Paul: Currently Assistant superintendent with a railway overseeing and having responsibility for all the rail activity from Superior, Ladysmith, Chippewa Falls in WI to the Twin Cities in MN. Prior I had worked at our hump yard in Gary, IN. Before that I had worked for 2 other railroad companies taking me from St Paul, MN to Green River, Wy to Decatur, Il. Covering various stretches of territory and industries there in. We live in Wisconsin.

Hilary: Teach high school and live in my hometown.

MaryBeth: Being a math geek, I used to calculate pension plans and explain them to retirees over the phone in layman's terms putting my Communications degree to good use. Now I work for a nationally known blood bank administering Compensation and all types of retirement plans.

Ed: We live in Indiana. for the last year, after spending nearly 10 years in Nashville. For the first ten years of my career I had various roles in corporate accounting and finance. In 2012, I made the leap of faith to get into financial services. I'm now a CERTIFIED FINANCIAL PLANNER TM with my own independent practice based in Indianapolis. I'm thankful that I did as I know I'm doing great work for my clients, and I come home every day feeling happy and knowing I'm making a positive impact on the world.

Annie: After college I lived in Davenport, IA and worked as a youth minister while going to University of Iowa for a music therapy certification. Moved back to Chicago and worked as a board certified music therapist in hospice care, continued education to use music therapy in child birth and become a professional doula. I am self employed - freelancing in both areas while being at home with my kiddos and homeschooling.

Greg: I went on to get my Master's of Architecture from Wash U in STL. I work as an architectural designer at a firm in Boston.

Megan: Class of 05, I'm currently going into my 16th year of teaching. I obtained my masters in curriculum and instruction in 08 from Concordia University. I work as a third grade teacher and have taken on the roll as grade level representative for the past 7 years. I have presented on various topics to other teachers at several district and county level conferences. I live in my hometown but teach for the second largest district in Illinois.

Marquis: Got my Masters in Higher Education and Student Affairs from the University of Vermont and now I work at San Diego State University as a residence hall coordinator

James: Hi. I'm living in Bloomington Indiana. I earned my Masters degree in Counseling and Counselor education (M.S. Ed.)from Indiana University. I work as a clinician doing mental and behavioral health counseling with Individuals with intellectual and developmental disabilities and a coexisting mental health diagnosis for a local agency. I also run local martial arts school and am a part time professional photographer.

Sarah: I'm going into my 21st year of teaching in the western suburbs of Chicago

Andrea: Living in Lee, MA (the Berkshires) and managing the marketing for an IT company based in Albany, NY.

Beth: I'm a VP of Customer Experience for a large company and have here for 15 years.

Eva: I have been teaching elementary education in Chicago Public Schools. I earned my masters in English as a Second language. I am looking to head back to school for a degree in Special Education. I have a part time job as a swim instructor and Special Olympics swim coach. I currently live in Chicago.

Emily: I work at the University of Chicago as Research Administrator in the central office. I review research proposals across the university to make sure they are compliant and approve them for submission. I also develop proposals for the Pritzker School for Molecular Engineering. I have a M.A. in Grant Writing, Management, and Evaluation.

Heather: Living in East Tennessee- Pastors wife and stay at home mom of 2.

Katie: I am living in Milwaukee, WI since 2015. After getting a masters degree in education and working in that field for many years, I pivoted to real estate and have found a lot of success at that, as well as the flexibility my family needed. I also help my husband run our family business of a video production company.

Christine: Currently entering my 19th year as a special education teacher, I did 2 years at the middle school level and am now going into the 17th year at the same high school. I have 2 Master's Degrees in different areas of education.

Rhian: I've been living in Wales for 13 years. I came over and ran my own pub for 9 years and now I'm a manager of a bed and breakfast. Currently studying to get my qualifications to be a mortgage advisor too!

Lindsey: Living in the suburbs of Chicago with my husband and our son. My husband and I co-own a remodeling business. Utilizing my business degree from MC in a way I never imagined!

Jennifer: I'm living in southwest Michigan We have been an active foster family for about five years and we have fostered over 15 sweet little ones. I direct musicals for Children'e Music Workshop and I love it! I think I met you when I was 16 at Lincoln Mall in Matteson, IL at a college fair. You convinced me then that I would fall in love with MC and you were right!

All of these are impressive, but I think the prize goes to Jennifer. Fostering over 15 children brings being an "angel who changes lives" to a whole new level. <u>Jennifer...you are my idol!</u>

CHAPTER 27---PARENTS AND THE SCOURGE OF MONEY

Over my 42 years, 90% of my work with parents has been a delight. They have been very helpful and fun to work with. I love doing coffee-shop visits with students and parents because it gives me time to learn what their concerns, hopes, and attitudes are. If they truly value education, if they are willing to "make it work," and if they really want a college like mine...then there is a chance the student will enroll. If the value, the will, or the want are not there...the chances decrease dramatically.

I have had parents and past-parents who have helped us at receptions (like Legge and other programs for incoming students), I have had parents and past-parents who have even helped at busy college fairs. Parents will listen more to other parents then they will to me. In their eyes, I am the "salesman" for the college. They love hearing from parents who are "satisfied customers" that my college is a good, safe, and valuable place for their kid to attend. I have even been at college fairs when, completely unplanned and unsolicited, parents of current or past students will stop by the table (as I am talking with a student and their family) and give a great testimonial. It really helps us recruit, and I am so appreciative of the parental support that we have.

One parent is actually a graduate of one of our competing colleges...and he has helped at college fairs for both Monmouth and his Alma Mater. One past parent still keeps in touch with me on a regular basis with news clips, websites, etc. regarding education in the City of Chicago and on a National basis. I learn a lot from him. One parent has such a close, tight-knit, and loving relationship with her son, that I thought for sure (on move-in day) that she was going to move in with him! One parent likes to come to visit the campus mostly because he loves our mashed potatoes in our caf (oh yes...and also to see his daughter). Hundreds of other examples could be given, but the bottom line is that parents only want what is best for their sons and daughters. In the Admission profession, we treasure our relationship with these proud parents.

My oldest son used my OWN words against me. As a long-time collegiate employee, I applied for, and was accepted into, National Tuition Exchange. This means that there was a list of about 350 colleges that my son could go to without paying a penny for tuition. Hallelujah!!!! Well...he managed to find a university that was not on this list (all his friends were there and he really wanted to be with his friends). When I asked him why he wasn't going to pick one of the 350 colleges, he simply said "Dad...when I hear you talking with parents of prospective Monmouth students, you always tell them that it is 'worth a little extra investment to make your child happy.'" Well...he had me there. Insert knife. Twist.

He was right. He had a great collegiate experience, he was happier with his friends there, and he is a very successful businessman today. We made the right decision.

Now if I could only convince about 3000 more parents of this. Not so easy.

Working with parents in the admission process can be a delight or it can be torture. Parents who "hover" over a student at every step along the way (we call them "helicopter parents") can be the most frustrating. I cannot tell you how many times, when meeting with a family, this is how the conversation goes:

ME---Jon, what majors are you thinking about for college?

MOM---Jon wants to be a doctor

ME---OK...Jon, as a pre-med student, which science major interests you the most?

DAD---Biology

Usually by the 11th or 12th question, I have to actually physically separate Jon from the parents to actually hear Jon's voice to find out what Jon REALLY wants (which is usually music or philosophy, right?). Working with parents is a delicate balancing act. We don't want them overly involved in the process...nor do we want them to be completely isolated from the process. Very seldom are we dealing with a balanced situation.

More than once I have contacted a newly applied student to ask them to have transcripts and test scores sent to us, only to find that the student does not even know that they applied! Their parents did their application for them.

I have also seen the other extreme. Students go all the way through the process (apply, have transcripts sent, etc.) yet, when meeting the parent (or talking with them on the phone) the parent says they have never heard of your college and had no idea that their son or daughter even applied there.

Most parent questions revolve around one topic:

Money.

Usually, any investment greater than $1 is an issue. Parents are willing to take out loans for things that can fall apart, decrease in value, etc. (like cars or homes), but for something that increases in value and can never fall apart (like a great college education for their kids), they are less willing to do so. This has always puzzled me. Don't they remember how expensive it was for Day Care Centers and Traveling Soccer costs? Are they just thinking that at 18 they can wash their hands of financial responsibility? Having been in their shoes twice now (I have two sons), and having taken out loans for both of my boys, I am even more puzzled. It was not easy. We made sacrifices. But the end-product was so awesome that (in hindsight) we made all the right decisions.

Now don't get me wrong...there are some family financial circumstances that are so dire, that students have little choice but to attend the lowest price institution (usually a community college), but in my opinion, this should be considered Plan B, not Plan A. Financial aid (scholarship, grant, loan, and work) is available, but not always close the gap. Students need to aggressively pursue outside (private, corporate, civic) grants and scholarships, but many do not do so. It is a work ethic issue. Searching for this money takes time and effort (there are some great websites for this like Fastweb.com and Scholly.com). It involves writing essays and doing interviews. Many students do not take the time or put forth the effort to do so. Many do and reap the benefits. This is my "secret formula for choosing a college" that I share with students:

*Work on your GPA. Take both SAT and ACT at least a couple times. The higher these numbers, the less it will cost for college.

*Apply to 4 private colleges, 1 state school, and a community college (use the community college as Plan C). Plan A is to go to a small private. Plan B is to go to a local state college. Make sure to request fee waivers from those colleges that require one.

*Visit all 6 institutions so you know which one you want the most. Ask good questions. Make sure they are the same "kinds" of visits (short group walking tour is different than an individual visit with an overnight component)

*Do the FAFSA immediately on October 1 (or whatever is the first date it is available) and list all 6 colleges on it

*Begin applying for outside/private scholarships as early as sophomore or junior year of high school. Here are some sites/sources to check out. I suggest at least do Fastweb...and even though it costs a little money, Scholly is one of the best.

Central Scholarship Bureau central-scholarship.org

Scholly.com (pay site but great)

Chegg www.chegg.com

College Board Scholarship Search bigfuture.collegeboard.org

College Scholarships http://www.collegescholarships.org/scholarships/states.htm

Learn.org Academic Scholarships https://learn.org/pages/scholarship_home.html

Dollars for Scholars scholarshipamerica.org/

Fast Web Fastweb.com

FinAid Finaid.org

Scholarships.com scholarships.com/

Scholarships for School scholarships4school.com/

UNIGO www.unigo.com

ScholarshipExperts.com

MyFreeDegree

Sage Scholars Tuition Reward Program

*When you get financial aid awards from all the colleges, your high school college counselor can help you compare them. If you don't get the award you want from your top choice school, it doesn't hurt to ask if they can give you more. Sometimes you can apply for more through "special circumstances." Get to know the admission folks and the financial aid folks. That is easy with the small colleges. The more they know about you and how much you want them, the better.

*You will find that small private colleges are usually very generous with their money, especially if U.S. News does not rank them top 40 (or so). Rankings really mean nothing. Fit is most important.

Over the years, I have noticed some disturbing tendencies in regard to parental views of college financing. The media, in my opinion, has really over-exaggerated the whole "student loan" situation. Admittedly, there are some students who take out way too much in student loans. If students take out more than an amount equal to the first-year salary of most jobs in their profession ($30,000 for example), they might be taking out too much loan. If they do an internship while they are in college, take full advantage of the placement office's services, get involved outside the classroom (to the point of holding leadership positions), and get good grades (all four of these things),...they have a very good chance of getting a job upon graduation. If they major in something viewed by many as impractical (philosophy, art, English, etc.), they should also take some supplemental "practical" classes (in business, computer science, etc.) and do some significant internships to increase their chances. With a "reasonable amount of loan" and a job, students are usually in pretty good shape. What happens all too often, however, is they do not take advantage of (especially) the internship and placement office opportunities. This, combined with too much loan, makes great "feature news fodder" for the media. This makes students more and more reluctant to take out ANY loans at all. In fact, having a small student loan to pay off actually helps a young graduate establish and maintain a good credit score.

CHAPTER 28---THE IMPORTANCE OF FIT

When I am at a college fair or visiting a high school, I take notes. The student usually fills out an interest card, so after they leave me, I try to put a note or two on the top of the card. If I talk with a student who, in my opinion, has interests and personality that would just be a "perfect fit" with the college, I put a little "PF" in the upper left-hand corner. Then, as I work with my inquired students to encourage them to apply, I work just a little bit harder with the PF's.

Emma V is a good example of this. She graduated in 2017 from Monmouth College as out top student. Upon graduation, she had about a dozen colorful cords and banners over her graduation gown. She was our Lincoln Laureate student...our top student both academically and in terms of extracurricular activities. Here is an article about Emma (written by Duane Bonifer from Monmouth):

To say that Monmouth College student Emma Vanderpool '17 is an overachiever would be an understatement.
The senior from Frankfort, Ill., is majoring in **Latin**, **classics** and **history** and minoring in **philosophy**. A member of the College's **honors program**, she has earned numerous awards and honors for her scholarship.
And now add Student Laureate of The Lincoln Academy of Illinois to her résumé. Vanderpool was recently named Monmouth's 2016-17 Lincoln Laureate based on her academic accomplishments and leadership on campus.

Vanderpool was the first student in the 38-year history of the National Latin Exam to receive seven consecutive gold medals, and one of her research projects was **published as an article** in the **Midwest Journal of Undergraduate Research**.

"It really means a lot to me to be a Lincoln Laureate because when I came to Monmouth College, I came specifically to study under (classics professor) Dr. Thomas J. Sienkewicz to study the classics," she said. "And in doing so, I was very much aware of the strong tradition of excellence I was entering into. So to be able to carry on that legacy in such a way is very meaningful to me."

Vanderpool plans to attend graduate school after she graduates from Monmouth and then become a Latin teacher.

"The real strength in the Monmouth College Classics Department is the interest it takes in its students," she said. "Not all students come to Monmouth with the intention of studying the classics, but the Classics Department here makes every effort to allow students to incorporate it into their studies. ... It's a great example of what the liberal arts is."

In addition to earning outstanding grades and helping lead several student organizations, Vanderpool was drum major for the Fighting Scots Marching Band this school year.

"Serving as drum major has allowed me to have a greater impact on students and share my experiences in a way that I would have necessarily gotten just as a senior or as an upperclassman," she said. "The opportunities that I've been provided here by all the faculty and staff are things that I never could have imagined before coming here."

I remember the first day I met Emma. She was the only student who came to see me that day at her high school. She said she was looking for a small college, not too far from home, that had a Latin Major, a Latin Education certification, and a marching band. PF. Search over. I think, within a reasonable driving distance, we are literally "it." We had all three. Thank goodness she loved our campus! I still have the card with the big "PF" written in the upper left-hand corner.

In my estimation, there is no more crucial factor in choosing a college than "fit." To that end, the most important thing for students to do in their college search is to VISIT. Personally, I won't even buy shoes by mail, let alone a college! Every college has a personality of its own. A student can read all the pamphlets, do all the virtual tours online, talk with Admission Reps, and they still really have no clue what the college is all about. I encourage students to do multiple visits, because they have to truly feel that there is a great "fit" for them. College are beginning to do a better job with virtual tours (especially due to Covid19), but nothing is a substitute for actually walking around the campus.

Fit is not just about majors, curriculum, and co-curricular activities. If a college does not have an engineering "major" it doesn't mean that its graduates cannot become engineers (some of the 3+2 programs that college have can help liberal arts students become very successful engineers). If a college does not have a law "major" it can still produce individuals that become top rated lawyers (lawyers can major in virtually anything). The atmosphere of the college, and what kinds of opportunities it can provide, are much more important than the majors it offers. Three of every four students' majors change (completely or a little) during their four years at a college, so if a student picks a college just because of its _____ program, they might be less than happy during their tenure at college.

Fit is more about:

"Do I feel comfortable here?"

"Are these the kinds of people I would like to be with for the next four years?"

"Can I 'see myself here?"

"Can the college somehow help me fulfill my career aspirations? Can they guide me in that process? Can I 'get there from here'?"

Remember this quote from the first page of my book?

Recently I posted on Facebook to ask if there was "something specific that you remember that I said during the recruitment process." Here was one of the responses:

Laur W

(you said) "If you couldn't be at home on your worst day where else would you want to be"... (as your) thought process for choosing a college.

· Reply · 2w

Me

Oh yeah...I actually stole that quote from one of our alums...

· Reply · 2w

Laur W

Peter Pitts It's a great one and why I chose Monmouth.

Great advice. The alum I "borrowed" this quote from is now a very successful doctor. His quote has really fueled my passion for making sure there is a good "fit" for students with the college I represented.

As an Admission Counselor, my task is to inform student honestly about my college, encourage them to apply and to apply for financial aid, and encourage them to visit campus. At that point, the college pretty much either sells itself...or the student ends up going elsewhere. The important thing, in the end, is not whether I recruit the number of students the college wants me to. The important thing is: Is the student happy? Is the student ending up where they really "need to be" at this point in their life? If the student is happy, if they are where they need to be, then I have done my job.

CHAPTER 29---STORIES FROM MY FELLOW ROAD WARRIORS

Just to prove that I am not the only admission rep who has experienced heartwarming, wild, and wacky things, I have asked some of my fellow reps (who will all remain name-less and institution-less to protect the innocent). These are in no particular order, but I would like to ask the reader to just sit back, relax, and enjoy these stories.

Rep #1 I work for a university where it is winter for the majority of the time our school is in session. Yes, we get a lot of snow, but we also are used to clearing it. Rarely do we have a snow day, and our students can easily and safely walk around our campus and town. With that being said, we do have a lot of students who snowmobile, snowshoe, ski and snowboard. Once I met with a student during a spring visit to his high school who loved snow and outdoor activities. A few weeks later (in May after all the snow has melted) he and his family visited our campus. At the end of the day, the student and his father went up to our bookstore and the mother came back to the admissions office to ask a few questions. One question was about financial aid. She told me that she though that our school was going to be too expensive because "you also have to factor in the cost of the snowmobile." I told her that many of our students buy used snowmobiles at the end of the season for less money to which she replied, "Yea, but how will that help him get around his freshman year." I told her about the free bus service we have through town and the number of students who have cars on campus. Looking completely perplexed she said to me, "I am confused. You told my son when you met him at his high school that students need snowmobiles to get to class because of all the snow." I tried desperately not to laugh. "We did talk about our snowmobile club, however that is an optional student organization. We have 24-hour snow removal here, so your son will have no trouble walking to class." You could see her stiffen. "That little bastard," she said. "It is going to be a long ride home." Swiftly she turned and walked out of the office, and as soon as the door closed behind her, our administrative assistant, who had overheard the whole ordeal, started to laugh. To this day, whenever anyone brings up snowmobiling I specifically tell them that they DO NOT need a snowmobile to get around campus and chuckle inside.

Rep #2 In my 25 years, this stands out as the most unusual thing that happened.

I answer our "search" emails. Here is an exchange I had with a student. Feel free to change the school names and/or amend:

Kid: What would I qualify for in scholarships? I have a 3.9 GPA. I got a 27 on my ACT.

Me: Thanks for your email! Based on the information you provided, you can expect a scholarship in the $16,000-19,000 range. Please let me know if you have any other questions. I'm happy to help!

Kid: I can get a full ride to the university of _____ and _____ University. YA $%# OFF. Your school is @#&. Go %#& a *%$. $#@# (expletives deleted)...

Rep#3 By the summer of her son's move-in, this mom had become one of my favorite parents. We had had long conversations many times throughout the year regarding the college, her son, and basically, just life in general. She was the "no filter" kind of parent who didn't care who she offended when she spoke, and I loved it. She always cracked me up, but she seriously outdid herself in this particular conversation:

Her son had received his housing and roommate assignment, and she had spoken to the roommate's mom about who was going to bring what for their shared room. The roommate's mom said they had an old, giant "box" TV he could bring. At this time, "box" TVs were still around but they were definitely not the norm anymore. Most college students brought the slimmer HDTVs for their dorm rooms, but the mom telling me the story didn't say anything, thinking she could let this one slide. Then the roommate's mom apparently told her they could also bring an area rug, because they had some shag carpet remnants in their basement. At this, the mom's exact words to me were, "I almost shit when I heard 'shag!'" I am fairly certain she was envisioning bright orange shag carpet leftover from the 1970s and all their glory!! It made my day, and I will never forget the phrase, "I almost shit when I heard 'shag!'"

Rep #4 I was in my first year of Admission and was sent to a community college on the south side. The fair was set up cafeteria style and I chose a table at the front kitty-corner from the Army, Marines, and Navy tables. I had a girl walk up, ask a few questions, then promise to come back after her class. She came back an hour or so later and started chatting with me again. All of a sudden her eyes roll back and she starts twitching and falls onto my table. In shock I reach out and grab her by the backpack straps -that's all I could catch hold of- as she started to fall to the ground. I'm panicking and looking around and no one is noticing. I somewhat quietly yell help. The tables next to me both look on in shock, not helping. I yell again louder and no one comes. I'm almost pulled over my table at this point. I look at the armed services guys and scream at the top of my lungs for them to get their asses over here. They jumped and came to my rescue. The girl was lowered to the floor where she finished her seizure. After she was okay, she was escorted off to the nurse or where ever the community college people took her to. Then I had a guy who told me he was some sort of director at the community college come up. He thanked me for my aid. Then he said, "I bet she stopped taking her meds again. She does this a lot. She doesn't like the meds so she stops taking them and this happens about once a month. Oh well, she's fine and no harm done. I'll talk to her about her meds." I packed up at that point and said forget it, I'm leaving and I'm never going back.

Rep #5 The first college fair I ever attended by myself was a memorable one. A student was being chased through the school by security and they caught him by pinning him down ON my college fair table!

During my first year in the profession, I presented to an entire English class during my visit to a high school. The presentation did not seem to go well and students were looking at me with glazed, uninterested expressions. The next year, I visited the school for a college fair. A bubbly senior came running up to me so excited that I was there for the fair. She told me that ever since the day I came to present to her English class, she had studied every detail she could about our school and it was #1 on her list. She told me she had never heard of our school prior to my visit and would have never considered it on her own. We worked together to get her set up for the Fall and lost touch after her freshman year. Fast forward four years, I ran into her on campus (we are regionally based so I don't often get to leisurely stroll campus as we are often in endless meetings). She was doing well and shared all the things she was involved in, how much she loved campus, what her plans for the future were, etc. She gave me the biggest hug and told me she has me to thank for helping her find the best place for her! It warmed my heart to know that she found her "fit" and was thriving on our campus.

Rep #6 I had a pleasant phone relationship with a mom of a prospective student. She and I had weekly conversations ever since the start of the application process in early fall. I finally convinced them to visit campus in the winter to decide if the school was a good fit. When we met in person, I introduced myself as her daughter's admission counselor. My very least expectation of this mother was the first thing she said to me, "wow, I thought you were white". As someone who is a person of color, I'm not sure if this was a compliment or an insult for not having an "accent" as I assumed she thought I was white based on our phone conversations. I wasn't sure how to react or what to say, but all I did was smiled at her and said "oh no, I'm Mexican-American and my first language was Spanish!". After this experience, I included Se habla español on my email signature so that families can recognize my bilingualism. As an admission counselor, I should expect the very worst when it comes to the interactions I have with families, that way I do not have to feel as surprised as I did, but this experience indeed caught me by surprise!

Rep#7 I was giving a tour at our campus to a family that consisted of a father and his son who was my student. Quick background on our college, it is a small environmental school in Northern Wisconsin, right on the shore of Lake Superior and about 45 mins away from Michigan.

While on the tour the father seemed "very relaxed" and was asking questions that had nothing to do with the content I was providing. On the tour, we were talking about housing, and the father noticed that some places had a porch available.

Father " Do all apartments have a porch for students to smoke"

Myself " Students are allowed to smoke cigarettes on campus, as long as they are 25 feet away from buildings"

Father "I am not talking about cigs, I want to make sure this is a safe place for my son to smoke weed. Do you know where he can find a good dealer?"

Myself, complete stunned " Actually in the state of Wisconsin it is still currently illegal to smoke marijuana "

Father " Yeah yeah, I know the speech. But you are an environmental school, and my son doesn't want skunk weed."

The Son" Dad you can't ask these questions!! Don't worry about the weed, worry about the housing!"

Son looks at me " Sorry he is really high"

Rep#8 In my position, we send out thousands of accept letters, but it is rare that I get to share with a student, in person, that they are accepted to our university. But once in a while, I do get that chance, and it's one of my favorite parts of my job. I will never forget one young man, who was a first-generation student, and had not received any acceptances yet. So when I told him that he was accepted, he was so elated, he started crying and got up to hug me. He then proceeded to talk about all of the ways in which he is going to work to be a great addition to our campus. That's the kind of student I'm looking for!

Rep#9 I met with student, his mom and dad. They are from St. Louis. The student is a highland drummer and the mom is a bagpiper, so that was their initial appeal to our college. The kid is maybe 5'10, 125lbs wet—scrawny dude! He had his major listed as Music, so I naturally ask what's your dream job? He responds with "I want to be Santa". I thought he was just being a smart ass so I rephrased and said what do you want to do with Music? Mom answers and says "he's thinking music education". The student responds with "...and be Santa." I just didn't get it. I continued the conversation and moved on, I was definitely going to circle back around during the wrap up. We needed to fill an hour on his schedule so I took them out for lunch. The kid orders a side salad for his main dish. (also very important for the story). I said (back to music education), "what grade are you thinking of teaching?" Mom replies with "he really isn't sure, but I'm just trying to convince him to not be Santa." I almost lost it at this point, because this kid really wants to be Santa. His mom was like "I told him he should get a business degree so he can own and operate his own Santa's Village. I don't want him to be like Beyonce who lost money her first year as a solo artist because she didn't know how to run a business." So at this point I am just trying to keep a straight face. I suggested he look into maybe a music and business double major or adding arts management minor to his major. His mom followed up with that they are really making a weekend out of it. They were headed to Dundee, IL to Santa's Village to meet with Santa, his mentor, to learn about future career paths...

CHAPTER 30---HEART-WARMING NOTES FROM MY "KIDS" AND FROM OUR ALUMNI

From time to time, I received emails/notes from students that I have recruited that really make me think. Sometimes they even make my eyes leak. Here are two of my favorites of all time (the first is written by a student at the end of her freshman year at Monmouth; She is now a college professor! The second is written by a student upon her graduation from Monmouth). These are a bit lengthy but well worth the read because of the emotion and great philosophical observations. Enjoy.

"So here goes...another philosophical thought from the empty vacancies of my mind. OK, so I lied. My brain is blown away from studying. I still wanted to send a big email out to all of you lovely, wonderful people I have come to call my friends, my compadres, mis amigos, and so on. I would like to wish you the best of luck as this quickly ending year comes to a close. Have we really accomplished anything? I certainly have; maybe not what I was expecting to, but what a year it has been none the less. I could never have guessed what I would have lived through this year if you had asked me on January 1. To say the least, graduating from high school and moving six hours away from home to go to college has been the greatest change. Which does lead me to an interesting little pondering...<u>the decisions we</u>

make in life may seem to exist at only that time, but they reverberate throughout our lives. Por ejamplo (for example), I happened to receive a brochure from Monmouth College in the mail one day and threw it on my pile of mail that almost every high school junior receives at that time. Out of mere chance, I applied to that school among six others. When I visited Monmouth on the way home from a family vacation to Florida (my first time there), I feel in love. By February of my senior year, I was settled on my decision, which made Peter Pitts a very happy man. So along came August, and I had said my goodbyes to Mom and Dad. Don't get me wrong, there were bad times, too, of course. I remember, shortly before Thanksgiving break, calling Mom and crying, begging her to come take me home. The admissions staff has warned all of the freshman we would, and I said I wouldn't...so much for that. I remember feeling so alone even though I was surrounded by people, and I remember being so angry and hurt I just wanted to hit someone. I guess my point is that I have made so many memories, and really all of them have been because of decisions I made before the memories could ever occur. Okay, so maybe you don't get that out of my rambling, but maybe you got something. I would like to leave you with this thought, to take with you into the next year and the years after that. People come into our lives for a reason, I am sure of it. And they don't stay there. Appreciate them while they are there; learn from them!! It has been a long time since I have seen some of my friends back at home, and some I will probably never see again. People change, they grow, and they go on different paths. Be happy that you have at least been given the opportunity to meet them. And I have decided, in my ultimate undying wisdom, that everything happens for a reason. I got that brochure from Monmouth College for a reason....it has brought me to this computer where I sit typing what I have learned to pass along to you. I figure, they may discourage cheating in school, but there is nothing wrong with giving hints in life."

Wow. Profound thoughts from a college freshman, right? Kids grow up and change SO much that first year away from home.

Hare are the words from a student who graduated in 2018:

Monmouth College over the four years has served as a learning environment for academics and equally as important, for personal development. The small classroom sizes have made the learning atmosphere so effortless because there was never a moment in which I was hesitant to just stop in a professor's office or meet with them one-on-one after class. Being a person of color on a predominantly white campus obviously has its own difficulties; but I think that Monmouth's administration did a great job at keeping everyone's sentiments in mind and protecting their underrepresented students. If there was ever a time that I felt uncomfortable in this area, I would never shy away from talking with the President or to the Dean of Students. The environment has always been so intimate, and I hope that it stays this way for future years to come. Monmouth is one of a kind in the way that the academic and social climate on campus balance each other out. And I think that is the true quintessence of a liberal arts experience."

Dan Cotter is one of our alumni who I have known since he was a Freshman at Monmouth. I missed recruiting him by only one year. While he was a student, I got to know him well. He lived very close to where I lived in Chicago, so when he was home on breaks, we would do lunch together, then he would help me in making phone calls to prospective students. Upon graduation, he worked full time for CNA insurance in Chicago while he was going to law school in the evenings. He graduated at the top of his law school class, was quickly named "top young lawyer" in Chicago, then eventually (at the tender age of 40) served as President of the Chicago Bar Association. He is also a member of our Board of Trustees. I am in awe of his ability to juggle so many things. How he does it all I will never know. He was so proud the year his own son chose to attend Monmouth. Here is what he wrote in Facebook:

"To those choosing **Monmouth** and their parents:
You have chosen well. I say that as an alum, I say that as a parent of a son who just committed to **Monmouth**, and as a member of the Board of Trustees.

For me, Monmouth College was a magical place. It transformed me from a shy, not very confident young man to a confident, more well-rounded individual. With very few exceptions, that feeling of it being a magical place is imbued in everyone who has graduated from Monmouth College.

I refer to my time at Monmouth as developing me into a lifelong learner. Monmouth taught me not necessarily the answer to a particular question or problem, but rather gave me the tools to critically think, to defend ideas, to explore subjects and questions and to be inquisitive and excited to learn more.

It is a place that I loved while attending and have loved and continue to love for what it has meant to me. It provided me the tools to be successful in various endeavors, it taught me to be adaptive and creative. It has served me well in two professions, accounting and law, It prepared me for what was ahead.

All of that is needed. But more importantly, it taught me time management, it taught me balancing the serious with the extra-curricular, and last but not least, it gave me a family that spans many decades - you will find that the friends you meet at Monmouth, including the faculty and staff, will remain a part of your life long after you graduate from this fine institution.

For me, I met my wife there. I met other people that I love and respect and remain in contact with daily. My best friends are from Monmouth. Some of those friends I did not know when I was attending the school, but the common thread of being a Fighting Scot and the magical experiences others have had like mine have led to friendships from the decades that I cherish richly.

As noted at the beginning, you have chosen well. There are a lot of schools to choose from and the process can be overwhelming, but you have found the school you will call your home not just for the four years you attend, but for a lifetime. I wish each of you well and congratulate you on making what I am confident is the best decision any of you could have made in the college search process.

Today and every day, it is a Great Day to Be A Scot!"

Profound words from a wonderful human being. Thank you, Dan.

CHAPTER 31---RETIREMENT

On January 6, 2019 I walked into our Vice President's office with my retirement letter in my hand. I chose this date to correspond with the exact day I began in this profession in 1977. My 42nd anniversary in the profession. He asked me if I was "sure" about this...and I said "150% yes!" Then we both had a nice cry...and a great talk. I felt so relieved when I left his office. I knew I was making the right decision...and that is such a great feeling! (Now that the Pandemic has hit...I am REALLY glad I quit when I did---posted 7/29/2020)

People always ask "how did you know it was time to retire?" I always answer "Actually...I just knew it was time." I wish I could give a better response, but at the age of 66 (at the time), it was as if this was just something that needed to happen. I want to write a couple books, I am publishing a website to celebrate all 700 small colleges in the U.S. (U3K4College.com), I hope to continue giving presentations to high school students and their parents about WHY they should consider small colleges, and I even hope (on a VERY part-time basis) to continue doing some college fairs (if they continue after the pandemic) As I type this I realize that I have "somewhere between one minute and about 40 years" to accomplish all of this. So, basically, it was time to retire from the "day-to-day"...and the stress that comes with meeting or not meeting enrollment goals.

After I told my boss about my retirement date (May 12, 2019), I "made the rounds" on campus. A few hugs, conversations, and tears later...they all knew!

I was anxious to post my retirement announcement on Facebook for all my FB friends, including about 300 of my recruits.

So when I got home from campus the next day, I did so. And WOW, did Facebook blow up with over 220 comments! Here is a sampling:

Chris J (former co-worker) I am so happy for you. Your tenure in that role is ADMIRABLE at a minimum....almost psychotic too! I am so glad I was "recruited' by you (to work for Monmouth). It's great to be a SCOT!

Bridget L S (recruit) Will you franchise a Starbucks next?

Adrienne G (wife of my previous boss; professional photographer) You KNOW we are happy for you!!!! You deserve it!!!! I can be your retirement photographer??? We can travel the world, visiting Starbucks' along the way- I'll photograph the journey, it will be amazing.

Danny W (recruit) In unrelated news, sales at Chicagoland Starbucks are expected to plummet this summer.

Do you notice a theme?

Between January 6 and May 12, I had a LOT of college fairs to do (28 to be exact...which is twice the normal number because another Monmouth rep in our regional office was out on maternity leave), so the time went by quickly. There were also three C.A.R.R. Luncheons. C.A.R.R. is the Chicago Area Regional Representative organization. At these luncheons, there were over 100 of my best admission rep friends from other colleges, and (between the three luncheons) over 200 high school counselors (many of whom I have known for over 20 years). The President of C.A.R.R., Mike, made an announcement about my retirement at each of the first two luncheons (slightly embarrassing...but nice). Then, at the third and last luncheon...WOW. Not only did they make the announcement, the C.A.R.R. members gave me gift after gift after gift. Over $600 worth of gift cards to various food and coffee businesses. I was speechless. NO WAY did I deserve this. So humbling. The most amazing gift was a custom-designed and printed (by one of my fellow admission reps) T-shirt...with the dates of all 28 last college fairs I attended...the words "Peter Pitts Farewell Tour"...and the very special words (taken from Monmouth's school song) "1000 Hearts Devotion."

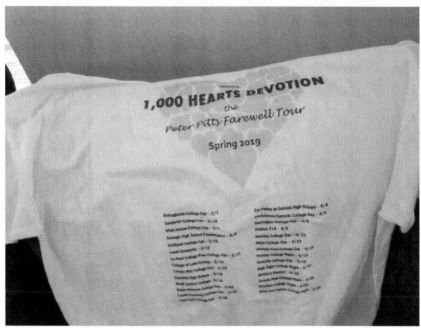

Then, at the last college fair of the year, my mentee Lisa Winker (I was mentor to her within our State organization) surprised me (and embarrassed me a bit) with a balloon bouquet. Those balloons stayed fully inflated months and months after she gave them to me.

Then came May 10. Two days before Graduation. Two days before the end of my 42 year career. Emotions ran high. The entire admission and financial aid staff threw a big party for me. I was expecting a few cards and a bunch of Starbucks gift cards, but what I got was SOOOOOO very special.

Backstory: I didn't mind turning in my ID, my College Credit Card, the College Car, all the Monmouth brochures and briefcases, but I did NOT want to turn in my key to the office. Somehow, since I had that key since the mid-80's, I kind of viewed the admission building as my home. I liked having access to the building whenever I was on campus. A key means "inclusion." Part of the family. You are home! I know that sounds silly, but giving up the key was really hard for me.

One thing the staff gave me is super special…and is prominently displayed on my desk as I type this manuscript. They created a wooden plaque, the wood taken from one of the buildings on campus (so I still have an actual piece of the college!!!), engraved by one of our faculty members, and an actual key to our office (not easy for them to get approval to do) which is super-glued to the plaque so I can never remove it. But at least I have a KEY!!!

Among other really nice gifts was something very special that virtually took my breath away. Nobody writes anything in cursive anymore, right? Well...the staff went around campus and had over 70 people write notes in cursive to and about me in a "diary" of sorts. This was a "tough read" that night. I went back to my room and began to read. I could get through about 3 pages at a time...then I had to just put it down. I went through about a half box of Kleenex.... I will never forget that awesome group of people I worked with. Never.

Two days after this party was Graduation Day. By that time, I was completely numb from emotion. I had so much fun at Graduation. I thought I would cry...but I didn't. Not even when the school song was sung. I just smiled and enjoyed. I was there to congratulate the graduates. They were the focus, not me. Thank God.

At least ¾ of the graduates had messages on the top of their graduation hats. This is the trend, of course! As far as I know, at least at Monmouth, faculty and staff (who also dress in regalia for Graduation) never had had messages on the top of their hats. Never...that is...until me:

Artwork on my hat was done by Stacy Lotz, Professor of Art at Monmouth. It is a work of art that I will cherish forever.

Peace out!

Epilogue---It's a job without end, Amen! (until it ends)

Yes, I am now retired---from a profession I just kind of "fell into". I had absolutely no idea, on January 6, 1977 that I would be here today writing about this awesome profession that I stumbled upon. I am so lucky, so blessed, and so appreciative of all the opportunities that this job has provided for me. It took a few years (and a few graduations) to truly appreciate the true significance of what I did. Working with these students, parents, guidance counselors, alumni, fellow reps, etc. has truly change me. This profession changed MY life. I have always wondered if Jack Fistler really understood how important it was for him to stop by my home that fateful day to give me a copy of <u>Mathematical Sociology</u>? (Come to think of it...I wonder if I ever returned that book to the Wartburg library...)

When students talk with their parents and their guidance counselors about careers, it is common for them to say "I like people...I want to work with people...I want to help people." The tendency is to inform students about careers like nursing, social work, psychology, and teaching. I hope this book opens up a whole new avenue of discussion. I hope students investigate this awesome profession. It is so much fun to have (even a small) influence on a student's future.

And please encourage students to visit small private liberal arts colleges...at least check them out!

Is Admissions a job with no end? Kind of---EXCEPT IN MY DREAMS. This is weird. At the time I am writing this, I am almost a full year into my retirement...and virtually every night I have Admission dreams. Talking to students, attending college fairs, driving from school to school...this is an almost every night script in my dreams. I cannot seem to escape it. This happens even in my "day" dreams.

It probably doesn't help that I am continuing, on a day to day basis, with college-related volunteer work, plus a little paid independent counseling. I have designed a website to celebrate small colleges (U3K4College.com), plus I have developed a database with information about all 700 small private colleges in the U.S.. I have also been giving presentation to "college prep classes" at various high schools within an hour of my home. I guess I never really want to stop changing lives!

I hope the reader has enjoyed the funny, sad, and powerful stories in this book. Every day is different in this profession, but it is, in many ways, a job that really has no end.

ABOUT THE AUTHOR

V. Peter Pitts

Peter Pitts recently retired from 42 years in the College Admission profession. He is originally from Iowa, and has an undergraduate degree from Wartburg College and a Master's Degree from the University of Iowa (both degrees are in Sociology). In his retirement, he publishes a website (U3K4college.com) that celebrates small colleges. He also gives presentations to high school classes about the benefits of attending small colleges.

Made in the USA
Middletown, DE
23 July 2022

69792151R00116